Also by Jane Holman

Pearls of Wisdom: For Your Path to Peace

Seeds of Self-Care: For Love and Serenity

*Light Ignited, Miracles Unleashed:
A Cosmic Blueprint for Your Miracles*

BEYOND THIS WORLD, FOR THIS WORLD

CELESTIAL WORDS *for* MODERN TIMES

BEYOND THIS WORLD, FOR THIS WORLD

JANE HOLMAN

Copyright © Jane Holman 2023
First published by the kind press, 2023

The moral right of the author to be identified as the author of this work has been asserted.

All rights reserved. Without limiting the rights under copyright reserved above, no part of this publication may be reproduced, stored in or introduced into a retrieval system, or transmitted, in any form or by any means (electronic, mechanical, photocopying, recording or otherwise) without the prior written permission of the publisher of this book.

A catalogue record for this book is available from the National Library of Australia.

Trade Paperback ISBN: 978-0-6458656-4-6
ebook ISBN: 978-0-6458656-3-9

Author photograph by Julia Keep
Typesetting by Nicola Matthews (Nikki Jane Design)

Print information available on the last page.

We at The Kind Press acknowledge that Aboriginal and Torres Strait Islander peoples are the Traditional Custodians and the first storytellers of the lands on which we live and work; and we pay our respects to Elders past and present.

THE
KIND
PRESS

www.thekindpress.com

We advise that the information contained in this book does not negate personal responsibility on the part of the reader for their own health and safety. The intent of the author is only to offer informative material on the subjects addressed in the publication to help you in your quest for emotional, physical, and spiritual wellbeing. While the publisher and author have used their best efforts in preparing this book, the material in this book is of the nature of general comment only. It is sold with the understanding that the author and publisher are not engaged in rendering advice or any other kind of personal or professional service in the book. In the event that you use any of the information in this book for yourself, the author and the publisher assume no responsibility for your actions.

To my guidance team, both beyond this world and of this world, your patience, insight and magic has been soul mission miraculous for me.

Be a bridge made of stars,
connecting heaven and earth,
for there is deep magic in this union.

CONTENTS

Part One
GOING BEYOND

Preface	1
Mission intent	3
Why are we here?	4
Minority group, large impact	5
Be true to you	6
Supporting our soul missions	8
Affirmations for supporting soul missions	12
Radiating for our world	13
Free will and destiny	14
Sublime failure	15
Immeasurable success	18
Aligning with the creative design for our lives	20
Influences on our sacred soul missions	23
Personal and collective soul missions	27
Establishing great connection with our missions	30
Challenges to our soul missions	37

Part Two
MEETING OUR CELESTIAL CONTRIBUTORS

Our divine guests	49
A. A. Milne	50
A. H.	52
Agatha Christie	54
Albert Einstein	56
Anna Nicole Smith	58
Aretha Franklin	60
Audrey Hepburn	62
Ava Gardner	64
Ayrton Senna	66
Barbara Walters	68
Benjamin Franklin	71
Bert Newton	73
Bette Davis	75
Brigitte	77
Burt Lancaster	79
Carl Jung	81
Carla Zampatti	8
Cary Grant	86
Catherine of Aragon	88
Catherine The Great	90
Charlie Chaplin	92
Christopher Columbus	94
Christopher Plummer	96
Clark Gable	98
Cleopatra	100

Coco Chanel	103
Colleen McCullough	105
D. H. Lawrence	108
Diana, Princess of Wales	110
Dolores Cannon	112
Edgar Allan Poe	114
Edward Mulhare	116
Elizabeth Taylor	119
Elvis Presley	122
Enid Blyton	124
Ernest Hemingway	126
Ferdinand Magellan	128
Florence Henderson	130
Florence Nightingale	132
Florence Scovel Shinn	135
Frank Sinatra	137
Frank Zappa	140
Franklin D. Roosevelt	142
Freddie Mercury	144
Genghis Khan	146
Grace Kelly	148
Gregory Peck	150
Harper Lee	152
Heath Ledger	154
Hiawatha	157
Horatio Nelson	159
Humphrey Bogart	161
Isaac Newton	163
J. R. R. Tolkien	165
James Dean	167
Jane Austen	169
Jayne Mansfield	171
Jesse Owens	173
John F. Kennedy Jr.	175
John Keats	177
John Lennon	179
John Steinbeck	181

John Wayne	183
Judith Durham	185
Judy Garland	187
Julian	189
Julie Campbell Tatham	191
Kelly Preston	193
Laura Ingalls Wilder	195
Lauren Bacall	197
Leo Tolstoy	200
Leonardo da Vinci	202
Linda	204
Linda McCartney	206
Lisa Marie Presley	208
Louisa May Alcott	210
Louise Hay	212
Mae West	215
Marco Polo	217
Marcus Aurelius	219
Marie Antoinette	221
Marilyn Monroe	223
Martin Luther King Jr.	225
Mary Quant	227
Mary, Queen of Scots	229
Mata Hari	232
May Gibbs	234
Maya Angelou	236
Michael Bond	238
Michael Hutchence	240
Michael, Singer, Songwriter	242
Michael Landon	245
Mother Teresa	247
Muhammad Ali	249
Napoleon Bonaparte	251
Natalie Wood	253
Neil Armstrong	256
Nelson Mandela	258
Nicholas I	260

Patrick Swayze	262
Paula Yates	264
Pope John Paul II	266
Prince Phillip	268
Queen Elizabeth I	270
Queen Elizabeth II	272
Raquel Welch	274
Reddy	276
Reta Shaw	278
Richard the Lionheart	281
Roald Dahl	283
Robert Guillaume	286
Robert the Bruce	289
Robin Williams	291
Roger Moore	293
Saint Francis of Assisi	295
Sean Connery	297
Shakti Gawain	300
Shirley Temple	302
Sidney Poitier	304
Sophia Loren	307
Tennessee Williams	309
Thomas Edison	311
Thomas Hardy	313
Tony Greig	315
Ursula	317
Vivien Leigh	319
Vivienne Westwood	322
Walt Disney	324
Whitney Houston	326
William Shakespeare	329
William Wallace	331
Zoe	333
Which beings are speaking to you?	335

Part Three
MY STORY, MY SOUL MISSION, TO INSPIRE YOURS

A power call to connect with your soul missions	349
Journalling discovery	350
Afterword	351
Acknowledgements	353
About the Author	354

Part One
GOING BEYOND

PREFACE

There is a world beyond our world ...
Open to this place filled with spiritual beings who desire to
assist our soul missions for the advancement of all. Infusing the
potential of the heavenly realms with our earthly living supports
our greatest soul mission activation.

Beyond This World, For This World has, within its essence, a desire to connect you, dear reader, with your soul missions: your reason for rising each day, your true soul purposes that give your life meaning. It is an affliction of our times that many beings feel akin to corks bobbing along an ocean, not really knowing where they are going and what they are called to do. Delving into the unknown is a beautiful thing. However, the magic within the unknown is far more accessible to those who feel a deep connection to life with meaning and purpose as the primary undercurrents. Being connected to our soul missions gives our lives purpose because what we seek is also seeking us. Magic is created and miracles arise from this union.

All soul missions for all beings are of equal importance, despite varying in magnitude of challenge and impact. Missions are developed according to the needs of each being and reflect the ability each person has (within) to serve the self and the whole for this lifetime. Each soul mission contains celestial wisdom as they have been designed for you (and most importantly with you) before you even came to Earth. Your missions are encoded within you, waiting for you to receive the immensity of your light to fully embrace them. Trust your own inner compass. It will always keep you focused on moving in the right direction for you and your missions.

Know yourself to know your path. Trust that your inner world—your energy—is always drawing forth more elements of your soul missions. Knowing yourself and understanding your inner world makes the outside world easier to navigate and more likely to be akin to your soul essence and true desires. You are the compass and the map, always supported by a great guidance system.

Connecting with our soul mission or missions allows us to live our lives with actions and experiences that align with our own personal strengths, creativity and desires. This, in turn, contributes simultaneously to the needs of the world. As Julia Cameron says, 'We change and the universe furthers and expands that change.' The singular and plural version of 'mission' is used interchangeably as many of us have multiple missions—some pertaining to our own evolution in consciousness, creativity and potential, and others reflecting a more global nature.

Your soul has a plan. Make the space to hear its call, even if it is just a whisper.

MISSION INTENT

Live with purpose, be intentional.
There is great power in purpose.

Central to all missions is the desire to heal, to connect with our love, and to follow what lights us up. Healing ourselves and opening to more love allows us to use our radiance to inspire and replenish the world. Our wellness enhances our soul work. Uniquely personal healing is a key component of our soul missions. As we heal and commit even more fully to our soul missions, we access more soul-serving light.

Be prepared for your increasingly powerful light to reveal to you any inner shadow aspects, that is, anything that needs to be healed and released so you can fully realise the potential within you and your soul missions.

Healing is always a part of our life journey and is an ever-evolving process rather than a destination. Perfection is an unrealistic state. It rarely exists in nature or in humans. Perfection is a point of view that is always open to interpretation. Our bodies are always expertly processing and healing something. Flow with the tides of healing. Trust in the brilliance of your body: the vehicle for your soul missions. Embrace all states of healing to allow peace to permeate your missions. Consider yourself whole as you keep moving towards wholeness. We all have our own unique healing requirements which change and evolve along with ourselves and our missions.

Although there are many commonalities surrounding our soul missions, they also contain many specific agendas. Some lifetimes may purely be about creating fun for self and others, or they may bequeath us with relaxation as the core mission. Your current life may be a restorative, regrouping lifetime following a previous lifetime of challenging, tireless work, possibly involving much work on yourself spiritually, physically and emotionally. As lightworkers, we have incarnated to discover our own power and light through the exploration of the full potential of our creativity, choice and love, combined with our innate wisdom and gifts. In undertaking a reconnaissance of the infinite potential of ourselves as beings, we are also exploring the potential for all of humanity, such is the interconnectedness of all things.

This writing experience has moved me further along the continuum from individuality to universality: a shift that, if made by many, would greatly benefit the whole. My intention is that you also lean into your power and influence as a global being.

WHY ARE WE HERE?

We all have a wondering, a curiosity, an inner quest, a seeking to know what and who we really are, and why we are here. Many of us sense there is more for us and for all of humankind. At one time each of us has probably contemplated, 'What is all this for? What legacy do I desire to leave behind? How can we create a better world for future generations?'

These questions are powerful connectors to our sacred soul missions, the blueprint underpinning what we are here to achieve in our lifetime. Ask questions regularly so that life can continually orchestrate situations and draw forth individuals to support you and your unfolding life—a life that affects many. Your life can then be lived from a place of purpose rather than chaos, as your choices will be in greater alignment with your soul mission(s). When looking for answers, look within and to the starry heavens. There is magic within this union. Become a living question. Ask daily, 'Who am I? What am I here for? What does life require of me today? What do I truly desire to do, have or be?'

Commitment is everything and universe will conspire on our behalf to line up the conditions and circumstances for meeting and activating our missions. When choosing to respond to life via surrender, question and curiosity, universe will work beautifully with us to send the guidance we most need. Signposts may appear in the form of symbols, messages from individuals, books, repeating numbers, lyrics and so on. Each sign is designed to assist us in co-creating our lives in alignment with our soul work. Trust your instincts; they are your greatest guidance for navigating life.

MINORITY GROUP, LARGE IMPACT

If you have incarnated within any minority group, then your soul mission will include elements of teaching about inclusivity, equality, freedom to be, forgiveness, releasing shame and judgement, authenticity, acceptance, tolerance, understanding and inner peace—and also embracing this within yourself. You are, in effect, re-inventing and re-defining societal norms and conditioning. Minority groups are simultaneously uncovering and creating awareness around subjects and choices that have been considered taboo throughout history, shining radiant light and creating miracle mindset changes within the masses. Look at the encouraging changes we are seeing in minority group representation in the film and television industry. This platform is bringing much awareness and change. You are bringing changes to the planet that have not been witnessed in millennia. Your peaceful, relentless intent to create change is working in extraordinary ways.

We still have a long way to go until all persons, regardless of colour, gender, sexual orientation and physical ability, feel fully witnessed and fully accepted in all facets of life. Small steps. Giant leaps. Transformation of great calibre is occurring through your efforts. You are re-wiring humanity in unprecedented ways, and we all benefit. Tell your stories. Write of your experiences. Speak your truth. Take us on a new journey with you. Our soul mission learning is more connected than we realise. We cannot unlearn and fully embrace what we do not understand. Be patient with us. Change requires patience and increasing awareness. In time, perhaps there won't even be a need for limiting terms such as minority or majority group as a greater sense of oneness and universality will prevail. Keep reaching for more until you feel complete and your soul missions feel complete—from this space you can always create more.

Throughout this writing experience, I have undergone some kind of metamorphosis. I'm coming to see that much of what I grew up believing was 'real and true' is quite the opposite. I've experienced a deep sense of destroying an old reality to create a new one—one that is more aligned with me individually and as a global citizen. Minority groups (for want of a better term) have played a considerable role in lifting many veils from my eyes and opening greater depth in my heart.

Although we live on the same planet, we each experience a different world. Whatever your experience of life, allow your wisdom to guide you closer towards the freedom of truth, speech and living. I also feel that many of us know what it feels like to be marginalised. Perhaps we perceive that we have belonged to a 'minority' group most of our lives, not quite fitting in with the more vocal majority, and instead seeing the world in a vastly different way. Different worlds, same planet. Whatever your experience, your wisdom is always guiding you towards the freedom of truth.

BE TRUE TO YOU

Our soul missions evolve with greater ease when we take control of the forecast of our lives. Seek to eradicate the white noise that can become a broadcast of the familial and cultural conditioning that easily influences our choices. It is paramount to know oneself, one's true desires and not be overtly influenced by the multitude of outside opinions. Life can then move us along the path that reflects our true vision and core values. Accessing our inner wisdom allows us to live by design, not by default. We get to express our soul gifts, talents and abilities, whilst our inner guidance supports the unfolding of our soul missions with the ultimate endgame of meeting even more of our true, authentic, loving selves.

Our missions all benefit from our authenticity. Being authentic means that we are open to the full expression of attributes, feelings and actions that desire to come through us. Something is always seeking to come through us, wishing to take form, because that is how life is created and how it evolves in new ways. This process of connecting with our authenticity is best supported by an open heart and a clear mind. For example, to create my best writing, I must be in alignment with who I am in my essence: a clear, open conduit for receiving the writing and receptive enough to live through the inherent messages to achieve the book's most authentic expression. Being powerful in life is tied to our willingness to be authentic, even if how this is expressed is vastly different from any current societal behavioural norms.

For many of us, authenticity has been a challenge because it is often influenced by, if not defined by, the world around us—even if this is not a conscious choice. Our missions require us to 'be free to be', expressing who we need to be and serving in the way that is most aligned with the truth of us.

Be authentastic (my new word) and life will show you fantastic!

Be something different and do something different to achieve something different.

SUPPORTING OUR SOUL MISSIONS

'The wound is the place where the light enters you.'
– Rumi

We all have the primary purpose of healing, that is, shining light on all the dark places within us. The places that are hiding our wounds, fears, stories on repeat, beliefs and limiting points of view.

Once we move into the freedom of wholeness and the accompanying voice of our true selves (as the ego voice, the imposter, has been given notice that it is no longer running things), we can receive the call of our soul. From here, we can lean into our intuition and determine where our joy and inspiration are found, further connecting us with the depth of our sacred soul missions. We do not need to 'fully' know our soul missions, as I perceive this is an unfolding process, something that is revealed to us throughout our lives in divine timing and morphing in new ways as we learn, grow and transform. Often, certain stages of our missions are withheld until we are ready for the next evolution of ourselves and our mission. This is most likely because we may not successfully be open to the full potential and greatest possibilities (or do anything with opportunities that are presented) if we are not ready for the next stage of our soul path. Divine timing comes into play throughout our missions, even more so when we are open to intuitive guidance and experience freedom from being vested in outcomes. When we fully connect with our soul missions, our life may not make sense to anyone else, but it will feel right for us and will involve intuitive leads that we learn to follow with greater consistency.

We have many sacred soul missions in life, for all the seasons of our lives. As we become aware of and release our unique, personal set of limitations, true alchemy takes over, shifting much in the way of our soul missions. Be a seeker; be still often to find those shadow aspects within that may be hiding the authentic you. Shine your brightest light on them. The stronger our inner light, the easier it is to connect with our truth and be led to our beautifully diverse and uniquely designed soul missions.

Many of us feel like we are awakening from a deep sleep, unlearning what we thought was true and real. We are becoming a part of a personal and global unlearning: uncovering 'unreality' to create our destined reality. This can often be an unlearning of enormity, including a total rewiring of function and belief systems. We are, in effect, challenging the reality we've had crystallised into our consciousness through years of conditioning.

'You must unlearn what you have learned.'
– Yoda, Star Wars V The Empire Strikes Back (1980)

We are beginning to let go of who we thought we should be and are instead leaning into becoming our true bona fide selves.

Give yourself permission to push the expected rules and roles aside to meet the greater you. It takes time, a lot of releasing, and a lot of bravery. It takes great courage to show up for your gifts and accompanying missions. Take comfort and inspiration in knowing that the rewards for embracing one's soul talents are gigantean for self and others. Move through your fears to find the freedom to creatively express all that has been seeded within you for leaving a great mark on life. Be determined to avoid allowing your potential joys and success stories to pass you by because conditions are far from perfect or you're scared of what you don't know, don't understand or can't control. Your soul knows the way and is aware of your greatness. Allow yourself to be led away from your fear and towards your true capabilities. We become magicians, releasing all the derivatives of fear that do not serve our soul missions. As something is desiring to leave your life, notice also what desires to flood into this newly available space. This is evidence of your power as a modern-day alchemist.

We can support our soul missions by acknowledging and giving up the program (that we may have inadvertently signed up for) of being the good boy or girl. Many of us grow up learning to feel safe and loved by being good. Choosing to be good reveals itself in many ways. We may have become conditioned to seeking praise and receiving 'gold stars' for doing or saying things that pleased our parents, thus 'earning' more love and associated feelings of comfort for being good. We may not have displayed emotions that made our adult carers uncomfortable, and we might have unwittingly continued this pattern in our adult lives. Adhering to 'goodness' may show up as choosing, often unconsciously, to adjust our behaviour and words to please authority figures. These feelings contain a degree of falsity as they rely on giving our power away to outside authority. Learning to be good often means we divorce who we really are to seek the approval of another. This approach means we live on very shaky ground as it is almost impossible to please everyone around us and still be true to ourselves. What happens to our resilience if we are out of favour? Worth becomes dependent on receiving validation from others.

Seeking to be good also encourages unrealistic and harmful perfectionist tendencies. Self-judgement can all to easily become a limiting default pattern as we often check ourselves over what we've said or done. We are human and often say things that could have been avoided. We are not robots. Not everything that comes out of our mouths is a perfectly rehearsed speech designed for peaceful, first-class interactions. You know you are stepping into your authentic power when you say something regrettable, acknowledge that perhaps it wasn't the best choice in the moment (giving oneself permission to not be perfect) and let it go. Most important is the letting it go, free of guilt and any form of self-berating. This approach promotes learning from the encounter. You will continue to step into being the best version of yourself and know deeply that all is well within you and therefore in life. Embrace your glitches and imperfections as they help you return even more fully to the truth of yourself and your wholeness. Your soul missions require you to love yourself and all your shades. You are a flawless diamond, so please stop trying to see your flaws in response to the 'being a good girl or boy' program. You will take the handbrake off your missions and enjoy their up-levelled unfolding if you can let the dimmed-down good girl go.

Throughout all experiences, be willing to be kind to yourself, taking all the time and small gentle steps you require to meet your missions with greater confidence. You can relax, knowing there is no set timeline and your missions will evolve as you evolve. Adopt the stance of curiosity, believing that everything is a learning experience guiding us to be, see and hear what is meant for us at any given time. We continually receive guidance to get us out from under our limitations, release our karma and move freely into our dharma, our destiny life, our sacred soul missions.

AFFIRMATIONS FOR SUPPORTING SOUL MISSIONS

'I am' statements connect us directly with source energy as we are claiming our true power and identity by invoking the 'I am' presence. Through these statements, we connect with the truth of who we are.

....

I am on this planet for the greatest of unfolding reasons, revealed to me in perfect timing.
I am still and quiet and hear the whispers of my soul.
I am divine remembering in action.
I am guided moment to moment.
I am surrounded by love and let love lead the way.
I am on time and on purpose.
I am love.
I am peace.
I am different and that is okay.
I am power.
I am connected to my inner knowing and wisdom at all times.
I am one with the universe.
I am gifted beyond measure.
I am unique, there is only one of me, and I do not have to be like any other.
I am a receiver of synchronicity and coincidence for guiding my life towards my missions.
I am continually open for signs that I am heading along my chosen paths.
I am a divine spark and I connect with this source as I breathe.
I am inspired, spirit moves through me.
I am turning the key to set myself free.

RADIATING FOR OUR WORLD

When we feel connected to our soul missions, we shine with purpose and meaning. We become radiant when we understand what we are here for, what we desire to get free of, and who we desire to be and create in this life. An undeniable wellness and vitality infuses our lives when we are connected to our soul missions. Without this connection, a sense of fear and frustration can permeate all our relationships and experiences. When we are aligned with our soul mission at a mind, body and spirit level, we are most powerful, content, and therefore living in a space that is most conducive to health. If we are disconnected from our soul missions, we can feel a sense of anxiety, unease, dis-ease and malaise. We can even move into addictive numbing tendencies like consumerism, social media overload, toxic relationships, alcohol and drug abuse, excessive busyness, looking for answers outside of us and judgement of others to avoid looking within. Being connected to our soul missions means we are more likely to be inspired and connected to love.

At the core of activating our soul missions is learning to love self and all of life. Fear keeps us disconnected from our soul missions. Love opens the door to them. Imagine the potential of a world where everyone was connected to their purpose and flowed with grace, thus activating their soul missions. Peace, love and creativity would increase in prevalence, releasing an undeniable magic and transformative power into our world in greater volumes. Our soul missions thrive, reaching new potential when we love what we do on any day.

'Let the beauty of what you love be what you do.'
– Rumi

This loving way of being draws all that is a part of your soul mission towards you—delivered in the right way, at the right time. You can trust this and feel the associated love and peace radiating through and outward from the power of your heart. What you feel in your heart is what you feel in your life.

FREE WILL AND DESTINY

Your destiny is always within you, always trying to emerge. Finding your truth helps to activate your missions and assist your dreams to come true because they are already encoded within you, waiting for you to meet them. What dreams are seeded in the periphery of your consciousness and gently calling to you? Your mission is activated in thousands of ways over thousands of days, little by little, step by step. As you live with intention and align your thoughts, feelings, emotions and actions with your soul callings, your missions are revealed. Your missions evolve and change as a body of great work throughout your entire life.

There is a myriad of possible ways to express what you came here to express. I surmise that nothing is set in stone and *that* is the inherent magic. If something is meant for you, if a dream supports your mission, your soul won't let go. You can trust in your own power to activate any soul mission. Life will rally miraculously to support your destiny. There will be lots of crossroad moments along the way and lots of free will choices and deviations, but ultimately, what is yours, what is calling for you, will find you.

I sit somewhere in the middle with my beliefs around just how much free will is involved with our soul missions versus how much is destined. I feel like the large moves, the soul relationships, are quite destined, because I have discovered it is very difficult, without some serious soul and life upheaval, to go against the trajectory of their unfolding. We seem to have free will around the small details, things that don't largely impact the sacred contacts and missions that are pre-decided in our spirit form. In my experience, if I've been leaning towards a strong desire or attraction for someone or something that may not be a part of a pre-planned soul mission, an inexplicable force veers me away from the current potential relationship or possibility I am toying with. I have found this particularly evident with romantic connections, which is evidence that who we join forces with or share a life with is intrinsically tied to our deepest soul missions. It also explains why many relationships do not get off the ground despite obvious love, attraction, connection and mutual interest—one or both inherently know it's just not the right time, place or direction. These scenarios, although often quite tumultuous, are magic in motion and evidence of a higher guiding power within us and surrounding us. Part of me desperately wants a handbook, a concrete guide for my missions and another equally strong part does not want to know, for she loves the mystery, the great adventure into the unknown. Without mystery, the magic possible within life is somewhat muted as the two are beautifully intertwined. The power is always in the present. At the same time, be willing to be captivated by the potential within the unknown. Knowing the future could potentially interfere in a detrimental way with the choices we make, hence why divine guidance rarely involves information pertaining to future events. Sometimes we may be gifted little glimpses of our future if it's for our highest good. Generally speaking, the future is firmly entrenched in the unknown.

SUBLIME FAILURE

The concept of soul mission success versus failure is an area I find particularly challenging. The concept of failure holds more questions than answers for me as it is quite paradoxical. For example, is there a sublime element to failure—in that, it is a great blessing? Does failure provide a way to move us beyond where we are currently functioning into excellence of a new kind? Does failure really exist or is it just an ego construct? Is failure just the way life moves us along a new path? Does it break us down enough so we can receive new information and open up to more light? Is it just before we are about to give up that we are closest to success? Is part of us afraid of the potential success—wanting it on one hand and resisting it on the other? Getting honest with self and connecting with inner wisdom and divine guidance is the key to successfully navigating a clearer path through life's vast array of questions.

Case in point, I have heartbreakingly watched a dear young friend put blood, sweat and tears into an endeavour for the last five years with no financial gain whatsoever and minimal personal satisfaction. Nothing at all appears to have worked despite great physical and financial resources being poured into said endeavour. This has been her lifelong dream—or so she thought. Is it just not quite the right time? Has her commitment to this dream been a distraction from what her soul is truly calling her to do? Is she not ready for what realising the dream would bring to her life? If she revisits this dream several years from now with more growth and awareness under her belt, will it be a different experience and outcome? Perhaps this is just a rehearsal for the greatness and wonder that is to come. Or is this experience preparing her for something else? One truth I do adhere to is that 'nothing is as it appears to be', as there is always more to be revealed below initial surface responses.

Behind this aforementioned dream was a desire to be noticed, to enjoy great wealth, to be 'someone' and to achieve a level of fame as validation. I must wonder if some desires are born in ego as opposed to our spiritual essence. Perhaps if there is repeated failing, it's time to reconnect with a new path—one that is soul-led, not ego-led. I perceive that when things are soul-led, there is greater ease and flow and, most importantly, a sense of peace around the endeavour as one is not vested in any set outcome. The pleasure is in the doing, not a focus on the becoming. One needs to ponder how the dream or desire came about, considering the motives and origins. Was the dream influenced by others? Has it arisen out of a need to fill a void created by an unhealed wound or to prove something to self or another? Has it surfaced out of a need to compete or to serve? Understanding self and motivations is an integral part of choosing when and where to invest our time and efforts. Successful soul missions depend on it.

Where I become a little stuck is with the old adage that suggests we can't fail unless we stop, that is, give up. Knowing whether to 'stay or go' in any scenario requires our deepest connection to our unobstructed inner guidance. Failure challenges us to our core and simultaneously opens us to new awareness and trajectory. Failure puts us directly in touch with any hidden wounds, ego-derived motivations, limiting shadow aspects and unresolved childhood trauma. These may be impacting how tightly we hold onto a current dream versus opening to a new dream for our highest good. On the days you may feel like you're going to break or fall, hold on! For one day, dear reader, you will know your worth in all that you do, regardless of outcomes.

Avoid allowing any perceived prior 'failings' to negatively impact your future directions and dreams. Enjoy your dreams as they are percolating. Take pleasure in the process along the way, the bravery, the learning and all the forays into the unknown. There is no necessity to experience joy only in the manifestation. Let the fun begin as soon as a new idea is seeded.

Enjoy the little buds as much as the beautiful blooms.

IMMEASURABLE SUCCESS

Success by whose standards?

Redefine your definition of success to create greater peace and contentment within your missions. If you are following guidance, doing what you are called to do with love in your heart, have a healthy dose of enthusiasm, have a desire to serve and make the world better in some way, then you are extremely successful. Turn society's definition of success on its head. **Ease the pressure to avoid missing the joy.** Popular consensus tells you that success is based on the money you earn, the house you live in, the number of clients you work with, the social media followers you have, the acknowledgment you receive and so on down the path of 'it's never enough'. Success often has connotations of competition around who has more, who has sold more and who has done more. All of this is open to interpretation.

Real success is not to be the effect of any pre-determined criteria based on competition, comparison or judgement. Real success is determined individually and involves maintaining a sense of peace with whatever arises; simultaneously maintaining belief and staying open to unexpected magic. One beautiful client session, one sale, one Instagram like, one painting, one book sold, one great friend, one sporting victory. What story have you assigned to only having one, two, five, ten or one hundred (whatever the number is for you) of something? Celebrate each gain without lessening it by deciding it's not enough. We need to move away from quantity, sales and accumulation as a determiner of success, otherwise there is no endpoint and only limited space for the peace from which our greatest potential arises.

If you have attempted something with fervour and love and it has arisen from the best of you, decide it is a success, regardless of the results. You are successful today and every day when following what brings you joy and contributing to the betterment of life.

Don't allow results to steal your joy or allow the ego to form negative stories about you and your accomplishments. When you least require success or accolades is the moment when surprising success arrives. Universe loves us to move into the space of freedom from outcomes. Liberate yourself from any patterns of belief in limitation. Seek the quiet truths regarding your success that are found under the misleading noise of the ego. Breathe into your peace and accompanying truth. Often, I feel we engage the ego to force our freedom from some lurking limitations. Discomfort contains magic as it 'encourages' us to release unhealthy patterns. We issue ourselves tests to see what we are truly ready to overcome.

The key to 'success' is not allowing results or outcomes of any kind to mean anything about you. True success is trusting what is occurring. Universe is always working to reveal more of us to us—this is the universe's definition of success.

Once your success is not defined by societal definitions, you are free to feel success in all your days. You are paradoxically more likely to draw in what society considers success to be—abundance of all kinds—for you are living through your love and peace as opposed to judgements around your enough-ness. **Abundance is evidence of the belief in your dreams.** Your dreams are signposts for guiding the action required to support your soul missions. Avoid deciding that success comes only from hard work or from something you have had to fight for, perhaps over a long period of time. Allow success to occur spontaneously or with great ease. Never underestimate or devalue your power to manifest, that is, your innate ability to connect with the creative energy of the universe to support you in manifesting that which brings value to your life and to the world.

ALIGNING WITH THE CREATIVE DESIGN FOR OUR LIVES

Trust in the timing of your birth. There is a far grander plan and design to your life than you can imagine.

Any time we feel inspired, it is highly likely we are connecting with the inner blueprint guiding us forward on our soul missions. **We've come here to meet our mission, to move life beyond what it was before.** This desire for expansion is beautifully ingrained within us. We can't disconnect from our soul missions even though life will take us on many journeys and often we will feel off course. Each experience, emotion and reaction exists to help us be in alignment with the many desires we have for expansion and the type of service we have encoded within us. Being in alignment with our missions not only elevates our spirits and enhances our lives, it also contributes to the change needed and the current energy and action required for our ever-evolving world.

My hope is that exposure to the soul missions of many beings from beyond this world, who are now blessed with the wisdom of the heavens (combined with hindsight regarding Earthly incarnations and an overview of current times), may help us to remember and connect more fully with what we hope to achieve this lifetime. When looking for answers, be curious, stay open and expand your belief system. You just never know where inspiration may come from—as has been my experience throughout this unique writing experience. We all have a desire for a greater reality. To meet this new enhanced reality, we must believe we can overcome all old beliefs and limitations, thus opening up to more. We can then connect to our inner vision and draw in the resources, self-care, synchronicity, creativity, teachers and attributes we require to meet our missions. Life becomes quite stunning when we discover who we can be and what we can generate.

Change the way you view life, and the
life you view will change.

Open yourself to co-creation with universal energy and guidance to bring forth the greatest design for your life and our evolving planetary life. It is in our best interests to be intentional with our living to support our creativity. Pam Grout says that every day she sets the intention to erase all beliefs, thoughts and emotions that block the power of source. Great intentions allow us to move into the space of being the difference (that makes an even bigger difference) in the world. Seek to be unlimited in thought, word, belief and deed and meet your untapped creative potential.

We are being called to share our soul gifts of a creative, innovative and emotional nature. To enhance your soul missions, discover what best opens the door to your creativity. Is your creative muse awakened through rest, peace, adventure, meditation, nature, art, connection or do you have a combination of entry points? **Our innate nature is to create.** Creativity brings contentment to our days and is an integral part of the contribution we gift to life. Hold on to your creations with love and lightness so they can find their own form of expression.

'As we are creative beings, our lives become our work of art.'
– Julia Cameron

I can't emphasise enough that all soul missions and their creative outward expressions are of equal value. We can't all incarnate as Egyptian pharaohs—we don't need that many and few people would desire to do so. The most powerful, conscious lives are often lived from the sidelines. Many quiet achievers make a loud impact.

Never question the value of your soul missions or compare them to those of another. There is always a bigger picture involving other lifetimes and great spiritual design. All roles played and missions undertaken are significant in their own way and in their own place and time. Most beings have similar requirements within their soul missions (variations of moving from fear and all its derivatives to love), but with different ways of growing, expressing and sharing the learning, transformation and consciousness.

There are active times within our missions and there are quiet times for seeding the new or reflecting on what has been. Our missions possibly involve much outward visible expression and then there may be a retreat into a simpler existence. For example, after I have released into the world the writing that is part of my soul mission, I may quite happily drift into obscurity, loving the simple life of nature, travel, self-care, home, movement, fashion, books, and loving and enjoying my beautiful family.

Embrace the ebbs and flows, the upsides and downsides and the chaos and peace within your missions. Return to your love and contentment throughout. Life is meant to be enjoyed with an overarching theme of love and peace.

Many of us feel like we have so much to offer but feel bogged down in day-to-day comings and goings. Often, we may feel that nothing is happening, nothing is changing. However, it is within these stages that much background work is being undertaken, even if not fully recognised or understood.

Trust that your missions co-exist with the ordinary. In fact, the ordinary is where they arise, giving birth to the extraordinary when you are ready, and life is ready to catch up with you. All you can do is just keep showing up as you are, seeking the best version of yourself and tuning into your inspiration and personal 'loves' as guidance for what is calling to you at a soul level. Create, dear creative being. Come alive to your life and accompanying missions one step at a time, just taking care of today. Be present, for you are the moment. Futurising blocks the flow of our energy.

*Author's note: If you would like to delve more fully into what is possible so that you can fully embrace 'going

beyond' during this process of connecting with your soul missions, Light Ignited, Miracles Unleashed: A Cosmic Blueprint for Your Miracles *helps you to unlock a life beyond limitations. This book develops your understanding of the true nature of how life works, (miraculously) introducing you to your miracle persona for bringing forth all that you can imagine and create within your life. It demonstrates how to allow the universe to work through you and your ignited light to create miracles and even stronger connections with your soul missions.*

INFLUENCES ON OUR SACRED SOUL MISSIONS

We are here for fruitful seasons in the sun.
Bask in your soul missions.

The soul desires the whole experience of life and welcomes the diverse influences upon our unfolding selves and accompanying sacred missions. In contrast, the ego only wants what it wants, and this can change on any given day. The ego is geared towards avoiding any form of unpleasantness (associated with a loss of control) even if challenging situations are gateways to growth, change or transformation. All of life can lead us to the sacred within our missions if we approach what is occurring with inner peace, grace, love and reverence.

In this writing, the term 'sacred' is used to imply reverence and respect for ourselves and for all of life, including our place within it. Embracing the sacred means connecting with the wonder, beauty, mystery and magic within us, the natural world and the unseen realms. When connecting with the sacred, one discovers there is a desire to be, create and contribute to life.

Make meeting the sacred integral to your living to bring magic to your missions.

We are all active participants in the co-creation of our lives. I use the term co-creation regularly to bring awareness to the fact that there are many factors that influence the unfolding of our soul missions. At a very simplistic level, because few of us remember the scope and grandiosity of our blueprint, we participate fully in the plan we have for each life. We reflect on the life just lived and on previous incarnations before establishing a 'theme' around what we desire to release, change and open up to in our new 'becoming' throughout our latest adventure on planet Earth.

We work with our guidance team and participate in decisions regarding our future family, birthplace and significant events within each new life, considering certain aptitudes and conditions we need to incarnate with to fully support our soul's deeper missions. I perceive it is partially a free-will universe, with much being out of our hands—more so if we disconnect from our inner guidance. Even though we 'arrive' with overarching intentions, life, the great forgetting, ego and our own day-to-day choices directly influence our life journey and trajectory.

Own that your choices, experiences and missions shape not only your life but the lives of others, such is our interconnectedness.

Learning to connect with our guidance team and our own intuition is vital in keeping aligned with our soul's sacred missions. Our soul family and other important players throughout our lives also have their soul missions intertwined with our own. Some characters in our lives act as catalysts for the upheaval necessary for us to stretch and grow. Others come in as karmic partners with mutual lessons to experience, whilst others come in just to love, nourish, support, guide and even mentor us.

> *There is a beautiful cosmic plan for every one of us. The word cosmic means 'harmonious order', and we are a part of this complex, ever-evolving order.*

Connecting with our soul missions means we have a greater chance of feeling alive, inspired, focused, motivated and connected to our higher self. This connection means we are more consistent in living a heart and soul-led life as opposed to listening to and being influenced by the ego voice and being taken down its associated rabbit holes of self-judgement, numbing tendencies, anxiety, despair, comparison or jealousy. We are so 'in our own lane' that there is minimal time for negative or untrue narratives. We make a greater contribution to self and others, and we are more loving, kind and compassionate. Our contributions count—they have a positive impact on those around us. We have inner contentment and peace arising within and radiating outwards, drawing in many positive experiences, opportunities and relationships. We are magnetic to our desires. Any time we feel inspired, it is highly likely we are connecting with our inner blueprint for guiding us forward on our soul missions.

Our past lives directly impact our current and future lives as what occurs in one life can flow into another. What isn't healed in one life rolls into the next. For example, one of my clients had a previous life as Peter the Great where she experienced death on a large scale. She faced great distress as bodies were not honoured or given a sacred parting from loved ones. This lifetime, she is revolutionising the funeral industry, encouraging people to consider, whilst still living on Earth, how they may best like to be represented and sent off after leaving the planet and returning home.

Many of us have an innate sense of dread, sometimes bordering on paralysing fear, when faced with opportunities to speak publicly. This can be due to a personal past life memory, or an energy carried through our ancestral line. Deep, unacknowledged and therefore unhealed wounds can transcend lifetimes. For example, many of us have been (literally) burnt at the stake for being the incredible, powerful healers and wise ones we truly are. Many of us still feel our throat constrict and our heart panic at the thought of speaking authentically. We risk judgement or abuse if choosing to go against popular opinion or accepted trends. A lyric from Taylor Swift's song,

'*I Did Something Bad*' (2017), 'They're burning all the witches even if you aren't one' moved me deeply, awakening an inner knowing and release and reminding me that, for many of us, it still feels like this is occurring in present times. As Swift sings, many of us can still feel the flames on our skin.

This lifetime, light up with your own flames! Speak up and show up as the 'stakes' are now in your hands. Be the person who 'did something' and said something. Remember: I am free. You are free. We are free ... to be. Choose to live from the heart and speak from the heart and your best life will dance to a greater beat.

Wounds of all kinds can be healed. Awareness sets us free. I recently spoke at a local women's organisation, and, to my sheer joy, there were no 'ill effects' and I enjoyed the experience. I felt free and so proud of myself for coming out from under this debilitating fear. In fact, I've come to realise that the very thing we fear most holds the key to our best living. I feel like I've been my own hero, swooping in and freeing myself from the past and the accompanying bodily reactions and conditioned emotional triggers.

Are you willing to undertake your own hero journey to discover who you can be and what you can achieve on the other side of your fear?

I believe that what we often fear is our inner greatness calling us to do things we may not believe we are ready for, taking us deep into the work we came here to do. In this scenario, fear *is* resistance to what desires want to unfold for us. Our soul missions require us to move beyond our fear into the potential and bliss of our lives. Say yes to your fears so they become your friends rather than your foes. We are true alchemists, capable of transforming even the most stubborn of limitations into something life-enhancing and beautiful. Transform, dear reader.

PERSONAL AND COLLECTIVE SOUL MISSIONS

Many individuals have personal healing missions and have also signed up for collective missions to raise the vibration of humanity. Our worldly missions often don't fully integrate into our awareness until we have healed ourselves, released our karma and worked through much of our own Earthly curriculum and accompanying individual missions. We undergo a plethora of experiences, seek to heal, and develop awareness and potential not only for us but for the sake of others who are connected to our soul missions. Our healing and learning then become a huge part of what we are here to teach and bring forth within the world. Our soul experiences support our soul missions and any worldly missions—if we signed up for them. Our individual missions are of primary importance and are inclusive of our double missions, containing the intentions we have for our own lives and for enhancing the collective experience. Activating global missions involves greater levels of divine support and intervention to actualise into existence.

Breathe deeply and connect with your inner guidance before perusing the following list of potential soul missions. Take note of any that particularly 'read' for you as a way of providing clues and markers for opening you to information around your own missions. You may like to highlight those that resonate with you for further reflection, perhaps through meditation or journalling. Let's see if we can stir up some remembering ...

EXAMPLES OF POSSIBLE PERSONAL SOUL MISSIONS

- *Learning to forgive*
- *Expressing gifts in specific ways to evoke change in individuals, circumstances or environments*
- *Meeting with other individuals to activate a particular mission that is interwoven with and supported by our own*
- *Sharing certain messages with the world that are pertinent to our times*
- *Surmounting personal inherited limitations*
- *Moving from fear to love (an intrinsic part of all missions)*
- *Helping a loved one or a karmic consort to awaken or heal*
- *Embracing soul gifts*
- *Identifying and healing personal shadow aspects*
- *Parenting self or another*
- *Connecting with soul mates and twin flames to invoke change within and for others*
- *Accessing personal power*
- *Connecting with nature to heal and awaken*
- *Opening to the power and guidance of intuition*
- *Being and receiving love*
- *Accessing innate gifts and wisdom*
- *Connecting with universal guidance*
- *Feeling good and feeling joy*
- *Tuning into and following what lights you up*
- *Spreading love, joy and light*
- *Learning to cherish being in a body*
- *Seeking and igniting your light*
- *Learning about life and your place in it*
- *Deeply knowing and understanding self*
- *Entertaining self and others*
- *Invoking laughter and joy*
- *Being happy*
- *Understanding and activating the power of peace*

EXAMPLES OF POSSIBLE COLLECTIVE SOUL MISSIONS

- *Bridging the gap between heaven and Earth by opening to divine channelling of information*
- *Creating works for the world that teach, awaken and open others to more of themselves via books, art, music, movies, photography and all manner of creations*
- *Being an advocate for nature and her creatures*
- *Developing life-changing technology*
- *Teaching one's personal experience of spirituality*
- *Bringing in intuitive guidance for opening others to their own wisdom*
- *Bringing forth new healing modalities*
- *Using gifts and knowledge to bring in the ancient wisdom of the cosmos for elevating Earth consciousness*
- *Connecting others to their spirituality*
- *Bringing joy through entertainment*
- *Creating books and films to awaken others to possibility*
- *Spreading light through large-scale media and organisations*

....

My intention is that these brief lists help you to celebrate all that you are and all that you are working towards. There could never be a 'complete' list as we as beings individually and collectively transform, create anew and up-level daily. There is so much more to us than we ever truly acknowledge.

Reflect on your amazingness every day to gift yourself the confidence to fully embrace and live your missions.

ESTABLISHING GREAT CONNECTION WITH OUR MISSIONS

A central tenet to best serving your missions is to become deeply connected with the universe's boundless energy, becoming one with it.

Connecting with universal guidance is key to supporting our soul missions. There are also many practises we can engage in on a personal level to support accessing our soul missions. Perhaps of greater importance is activating certain conditions 'within' that assist us in unlocking our own personal blueprint.

Highlight some of the states and practises below that most resonate with you as starting points for establishing greater awareness and connection to your soul missions. Choose one (or several) each day as a focus for your energy. Intent is everything and more powerful than we often acknowledge.

- *Journal with oracle cards to help you open to your soul purpose. Ask a question before drawing a card and then record any insights that flow through to you in relation to the card.*
- *Surrender to what is meant for you and, in doing so, allow the star power that creates worlds to flow through you.*
- *Let your heart lead first, aligning your mind with your intuition. Our intuition leads us to share our gifts, expressing the truth of ourselves and our wisdom for the betterment of all. We begin to create waves of consciousness and the potential for transformation not just for self but for many.*
- *Stay open to signs, symbols, images, synchronicity and seemingly random coincidences and experiences—this is universal guidance in motion.*

- *Place your hand on your heart and the other on a tree. Ask the tree to share wisdom with you for enhancing and expanding your soul missions.*
- *See obstacles, rejection or failure of any kind as simply the universe assisting you to question your choices, re-direct focus, enhance desire, re-route for a more favourable outcome or to encourage stronger alignment with a soul mission.*
- *Believe deeply that life is conspiring to help you make connections with your core missions.*
- *Ask questions to actively seek remembering who you are at a deeper level—our soul knows why we have incarnated at this time, but our mind may have temporarily forgotten.*
- *Open up to the possibility that you have a role to play at a collective level.*
- *Seek to come out from under all limitations, wounds and conditioned viewpoints to discover soul gifts to help support your missions.*
- *Move through life with intention rather than reaction. Life responds to what we focus on. Focus well.*
- *Indulge in daily practices that allow you to connect with and hear the quiet whispers of your soul ... perhaps meditation, time in nature, energy healing or journalling inquiry work.*
- *Commit to living a heart-led rather than ego-led life.*
- *Be in alignment with your higher self to hear guidance.*
- *Embrace your natural talents. We arrive on planet Earth with many of the talents and abilities we require to activate our missions. What comes naturally to us is often indicative of a potential gift for use within our missions.*
- *Work out what you love doing. Our soul missions are intrinsically linked to what brings us joy.*
- *Trust that miracles are your birthright.*
- *Honour your wisdom above all else.*
- *Seek work that inspires you. Our soul missions are linked to the work and careers that we are drawn to.*

- *Spend time in water and in nature where insight often just drops in.*
- *Meditate to open up to inner knowing and divine guidance.*
- *Be curious about all that life presents and be non-resistant to what is unfolding.*
- *Meet your world with wonder and love in your heart.*
- *Embrace the limitless possibilities within the unknown.*
- *Trust that activating soul missions is substantially based on divine timing and personal readiness. For example, my book writing journey started one morning totally out of the blue with no previous thought of being an author. The idea for 'Pearls' and much of the premise and structure came streaming through my awareness. Hindsight is a wonderful thing. Life had been preparing me to be an author for decades, even if I did not know it.*
- *Co-create, balancing surrender with action.*
- *Be brave and vulnerable. Our purpose and missions require our courage.*
- *Know that sometimes the things we fear hold clues to our missions. Part of us senses what is coming (as we are so intuitive) and we can be 'resistant' as it's not time and we are not ready. Remember that the universe only gives us what we can handle. My greatest fear—being seen and heard and sharing my voice—plagued me my whole life until I dived into it headfirst. It still 'bites' occasionally and has me withdrawing into my safe little shell, but that is okay too. We cannot be always 'on'.*
- *Back yourself more than you back anyone else. Trust that when you do, you become the best version of yourself and contribute amazing things, so it's not selfish.*
- *Face your own unique set of fear paradigms.*
- *Love yourself unconditionally.*
- *Wrap yourself in the warmth of worthiness.*
- *Have no expectations of others, only self.*

- *Spend your time and energy where people see you and love you. Let all others go.*
- *Learn your lessons in Earth school to vanquish your karma and live from dharma.*
- *Manage your ego, knowing it is not you and that it always tells you the opposite of the truth.*
- *Serve, contribute, give and receive.*
- *Awaken to the truth of yourself and life.*
- *Care for yourself first and others second.*
- *Connect with your true essence through nature.*
- *Learn the power of vulnerability to invoke courage and greatness.*
- *Be free of the effect of the opinions of others.*
- *Seek guidance to awaken and up-level, knowing what is true for you at the same time.*
- *Listen to your body and your inner guidance to heal.*
- *Seek spiritual connection as a natural part of your journey through life.*
- *Believe in the impossible and in magic and miracles.*
- *Unlock your ancient wisdom.*
- *Embrace oneness as opposed to separateness.*
- *Focus on your individual path and simultaneously be aware of the collective energy.*
- *Rely on yourself and your truth more than you rely on others.*
- *Value exploration of self rather than focusing on what others are doing.*
- *Take responsibility for the truth that our thoughts and emotions have power.*
- *See oneself as a global citizen, and not just concerned with one's own small pond.*
- *Be comfortable with your intuitive guidance when it is counter to the ego meanderings or vocal dominant opinion.*
- *Embrace new modes of self-care to heal and connect with the peace that opens you to love and your true essence.*

- *Follow your own truth, be the leader in your own life.*
- *Seek support and great mentors and simultaneously trust yourself.*
- *Remove the veils of illusion. See the truth of yourself and in all of life.*
- *Have faith in the grand divine plan.*
- *Embrace daily remembering that you are a cosmic being having an Earthly experience.*
- *Know that all that appears in the external world is birthed within.*
- *Be undisturbed by life to become free of disturbances that come between you and your soul mission.*
- *Excavate the inner shadow aspects to create the space for the light to flow in, opening to your love and cosmic love.*
- *Establish contact with your spiritual guidance team.*
- *Be vulnerable as up-levelling requires bravery, risk-taking and uncomfortableness.*
- *Make nature your friend, messenger and healer.*
- *Learn to advance and retreat in life. Go out into life to meet your triggers, reactions and limiting shadow aspects and then retreat into your own sanctuary to process what you've learned about yourself, for you. It's never actually about anyone else.*
- *Weave the sacred into all your days.*
- *Gaze upon all your life with wonder.*
- *Be in awe of you.*
- *Remember your true essence and be 'that', for it will draw to you all that you require for successful soul missions.*
- *Change your FOMO into JOMO—the joy of missing out! Do we really miss out or are we expertly (with universal guidance) missing out on what is not meant for us or not in alignment with who we are becoming? Trust in the plan for yourself and your life. Focus on the joy of your own pursuits and activities instead of what 'others' may potentially be doing. Embrace 'me time' to create experiences that nourish and inspire you.*

Consider the following journalling questions to further engage with your soul missions. Lean into your interests because they contain the clues and codes to unlocking your mission.

- What inspires you?
- What captivates your interest?
- What section of the library or bookstore draws your attention?
- What podcasts do you listen to?
- What forms of self-care call to you?
- What did you enjoy doing as a child?
- What are your secret dreams and desires?
- What would you love to do and get paid for?
- If you could impact the world, what would you change?
- What do you love discussing?

Make your soul and your wisdom the greatest guiding force in your life. Connect with your essence, for your essence is everything—it holds the key to your destiny.

Opportunities and possibilities arise when we are intentional with our living, not from a place of control, but from the reciprocal dance of action and surrender. Many of us are triggered so often by all and sundry that we are distracted from our core mission. Our destiny leading us towards our soul mission is always there, always trying to emerge, but we are so distracted with all that is external to us that we can't hear the whispers of our soul. Heal all that is in the way of the truth of you emerging. Get quiet, be still, listen.

Our soul missions are enhanced by our willingness to embrace change. Be open to change. Seek change. Become the change you seek. Invite change to the party. Become a shapeshifter, morphing into new versions of yourself as you desire. Freely move into new areas, locations and roles as required. Adopt a 'catch me if you can' persona—be unlimited in how you evolve and how you express this. Be transient. Be a gypsy if it serves you, your heart and your soul missions. It's okay to change your mind or direction at any time. Wear life and situations lightly, so if you hear a great new call, you can answer it. Consistency isn't a criterion for success. **Allow spontaneity and the unpredictability and power of change to be a part of your living.**

ESSENTIAL THINGS TO AVOID THAT HINDER OUR SOUL MISSIONS:

- *Worrying more about what others think as opposed to what we like to do and be.*
- *Channelling energy into worry rather than using this power to create our lives.*
- *Conforming to societal norms.*
- *Avoiding shadow work and therefore not fully healing enough to be open to receiving our light and soul guidance.*
- *Fear, fear, fear—the great progress blocker. Do it anyway!*
- *Not feeling worthy of your dreams.*
- *Resisting your intuitive guidance in favour of listening to the ego.*
- *Being stuck in cycles of karma, where not receiving the lessons or not being able to forgive and let go of resentment keeps us away from stepping into our dharma: destiny life, soul purposes and missions.*
- *Not taking adequate care of our physical vehicle for this lifetime. Our bodies require great nutrition, hydration, quality sleep, sunlight, grounding, energy healing and movement to truly thrive, allowing us to be healthy, present and open to receive where life is calling to us.*

CHALLENGES TO OUR SOUL MISSIONS

Have you ever had the experience of nothing 'seeming' to go right in life?

We may be rejected by a love interest, miss out on a job we applied for, not get the house we had set our sights on, not receive an invite to an event we felt we must be at, not have someone respond to a phone call and so on and so on. **Often, when things appear to be working against us, the universe is actually working for us.** The things that don't work out aren't meant to work out as they are not for us. They are not in alignment with our destined path, the one connecting us with our soul mission. Rejection of any kind is asking us to look in a new direction, to consider other options, to look at a situation differently, to take stock, to get quiet, to reflect and to listen to the callings of our soul. Embrace disappointment as a re-alignment mechanism. Each failure takes us closer to the success meant for us. Each time we fall, we learn, we reflect and we therefore up-level and transform self or a situation in some way. If we are disappointed in anything that is occurring for us, it means we have grand plans and desires, a need to expand or transform in some way. I'm sure the butterfly in the cocoon experienced great discomfort before emerging as her miraculous new self. Our discomfort is often an indicator of alchemy in motion. Celebrate this transitional state. Be in awe of the unknown magic that is brewing in the unseen realms.

Our feelings can come with their own challenges. At times, they can feel insurmountable. Our emotional state contains wisdom for us. Perhaps a strong emotional reaction is an indicator that we have strayed from our desired soul path.

If you are feeling anxious, your soul might be attempting to catch your attention. Most likely it has a message for you, something your soul deeply wants you to know, change or release to move forward into the space for receiving the next steps along the way in your soul journey. Anxiety can also be the call to heal, to face the shadow aspects, to nurse the wounds back to wholeness, to appease your inner child, to release the limitations and points of view that are keeping you disconnected or misaligned with your soul missions.

Negative emotional states (over long periods of time) can also indicate we are out of alignment with our missions. When we are 'on purpose', we generally have a great sense of vitality, inspiration and motivation. We are highly creative when on track and connected with our missions. Depression, apathy, lack of motivation and intense anger can indicate things are not quite right in our world. There may be unmet desires and places where we are out of purpose and out of alignment. Our souls are not lit up about our current choices regarding our relationships, living situations, chosen careers or even friendship groups. Something needs to change for us to recalibrate, reroute and reconnect with the truth of us, where we desire to be and what we require in our lives.

If we don't listen to the messages within our moods, we run the risk of existing at a low frequency over extended periods—weeks, months or longer. High vibrational states are everything. They are paramount for drawing in all that we require to be on track and connected with the callings of our soul to actualise our many life missions.

You may like to read *Light Ignited, Miracles Unleashed* if you are struggling to live in a high vibrational state and feel disconnected from your light and miracles.

Our soul missions rarely flow with ease until we as beings become more aligned with the energy of our missions, which is usually when purpose, passion and the desire to serve intermingle. Obstacles and challenges often present themselves regularly along the way. Sometimes this is because personal growth is needed to meet the demands of a particular aspect of our missions. It could also mean that the timing is not quite right and we need to pause for a while. Obstacles could also mean we are being tested. Do we have the desire and commitment to carry out and be what is required? Obstacles can fuel our determination as we realise how much we truly want something. Tuning into our inner guidance is important with all forms of obstacles to determine what is really going on. An obstacle could also be asking us to consider an alternate cause of action. Anything that challenges current comfort zones means we are stretching and expanding what is possible within us and for our soul missions.

Enjoy the multi-faceted nature of living through your soul missions.

Open your awareness to anything that may be keeping your missions at bay. You deserve the best that life has to offer. Trust that all experiences are deeply interwoven within the highest plan for your life: your soul mission.

Part Two

MEETING OUR CELESTIAL CONTRIBUTORS

Allow the soul missions of these otherworldly contributors to assist you in remembering and activating your own soul missions.

Recording the messages of each non-physical being (who has previously lived on Earth) required me to access another aspect of my soul mission: channelling. Channelling is one of the ways celestial beings communicate with our world. Throughout the channelling process, I perceive that I am being attuned, re-wired and up-levelled to receive guidance to benefit others as well as myself. I am, in effect, raising my vibration to the highest point for receiving their messages. The non-physical beings are simultaneously lowering their frequencies to a level I can 'hear', allowing me to process what wishes to come through me, for us. I am bringing insights from higher consciousness into a language and format (within my personal referencing system) that can be received in our Earthly realm.

The arrival of these amazing, eclectic contributors called for my most open heart and my most open mind. It also required much letting go of the past and my accompanying perceptions, with a need to acknowledge the influence of how 'history' has portrayed each individual. There are always multiple versions of one event and one life. I experienced a huge range of contrasting emotions whilst channelling each contribution for this book: awe, deep respect, cold (truth-indicating) shivers and shifts in awareness. I embraced forgiveness, universal thinking and divine 'eyes' to see beyond existing perceptions. I also needed to release much preconceived judgement. Initially, I admit I met some contributors with feelings of 'Ah' and 'Oh no!'. However, almost simultaneously, I was gifted with the bigger picture of what each life had been about.

These polarising lives were often catalysts for great change. What arose out of the seemingly chaotic negativity was the call to humanity to never allow atrocity, pain and suffering of such magnitude to ever prevail again in modern times. Each contributor created much revelation within me, for us.

I suggest focusing more on the message of each celestial contributor rather than the significance of who they were in their former life. They do not seem to make their 'stories' significant, focusing instead on the learning within their soul missions. Many have made questionable choices and ask that we learn from their misguided decisions. They appear to take full responsibility for their actions and have opened to the learning within their experiences.

When reading all celestial contributions, bear in mind that each being's truth (as it is for us) is deeply impacted by a unique blend of the personal experience of life, combined with inner motivations and innate personality traits. Added to this (especially for our guest contributors) is divine hindsight and beingness. Just as on Earth, I surmise that 'beyond this world' there are both commonalities and differences regarding individual perceptions of various scenarios. Uniquely personal interpretation can change at any moment in response to the variable nature of life and ever-increasing awareness. It is expansive to experience opposing viewpoints as we are then challenged to tune into our personal knowing as a point of reflection for potential learning. Like us, our celestial contributors are continuing to evolve and develop their own understanding of self and life. They do not ask us to align with their respective viewpoints but instead share their wisdom with the intent of deepening our own wisdom, encouraging us to lean even more fully into our own truth and accompanying authenticity. Remember, your truth is the ultimate truth for you. Many diverse truths expand consciousness in a myriad of ways. Life is a delicious mix of contradictions, opposing viewpoints and paradoxes. Differing viewpoints when approached via a stance of curiosity and openness to growth allow us to see what may previously have been unseen. Difference is a gift to evolving life.

Each life has value and impact—some more so than others at various times in history. Each 'guest' came with compassion in their hearts, a desire to be understood, and to teach from a place where wisdom was gained from their Earthly life and missions, both in the 'positive' and 'negative' events and consequences within their lives. All events are open to interpretation. I was reminded equally of the power of the collective and the power of a single life, the ripple effects that can flow for eternity. Ripple well, dear reader, perhaps even creating tsunamis of consciousness and positive change.

Your challenge, your choice:
Be inspired by these beings to connect with and create greater awareness and receptivity towards your soul missions to activate the greatest representation of yourself in this lifetime. We are all here to create a better world, leaving behind something greater than we have experienced and witnessed in this Earthly incarnation.

>**Author's Note: Some beings chose to represent themselves without use of their full names, just a first name, choosing not to be defined by their Earthly name. Their contribution, their choice. I haven't generally included each contributor's country of origin as they are all global citizens.*

....

Allow the life lessons and all the experiences, actions and choices within the unique spectrum of light and dark portrayed within our guests to assist your understanding of the bigger picture and the grand plan for your own life. Let the soul missions of our celestial visitors help you to activate and understand the power and significance of your personal missions. Enjoy and embrace their generous gifts of wisdom and insight. Allow their words to enhance your understanding of life and your place and purpose within it.

We are beyond this life.
Our reach is eternal.
Bring this power to Earth.

Prepare to be uplifted and enlightened as you successfully traverse these pages with love in your heart, openness in your mind and the flowering of new wisdom within your ever-blooming soul. Enjoy connecting with those who have gone before us, paving the way for us via their unique lifetime missions to help us acknowledge, understand and activate our own unique soul purposes and missions. I hope the enormity of our lives, and the power and potential we possess to enhance life and transform self and others shines through for you as it did for me.

The contribution of each being is structured to lead the reader deeply into their own soul wisdom. There is an *introductory message* to tune the reader into the essence of each guest contributor followed by a brief overview of each being's *specific soul missions*. Our celestial contributors (like us) have very long soul mission lists. This is because missions change and evolve to some degree throughout the decades to support our life stages and the inherent transformation, both planned and unplanned. Included here are abridged lists pertaining to the central themes of each soul mission.

Be prepared to open to soul missions that resonate with you, and that create an awareness within you regarding your own purpose, mission and destiny. Like us, most of the contributors have multiple missions, many of a personal nature and others pertaining to greater global significance. All missions are equally important and all contribute to the whole in exactly the way they are meant to, even if we don't fully understand the bigger picture. Next is some *guidance for today* to help us narrow our focus to something achievable in the present, and for enhancing our consciousness, awareness and current soul purposes.

Hopefully you will recognise an untapped or unexplored aspect of yourself, thus engaging more deeply with your potential via these celestial messages, and further encouraging reflection on what you may be successfully embracing. In doing so, you acknowledge the greatness of you. Your worth is all powerful in giving yourself subconscious permission to embrace your missions. Through absorbing these messages, you will lean into looking beyond your current circumstances as a bigger picture emerges. In receiving the energy of each contributor, you will find yourself opening to more of you and some next steps in your journey. Throughout this experience, keep honouring yourself in your heart, reflecting on what you've achieved already, encouraging further trust in yourself and even greater activation of your soul mission.

Lastly, *the choice* section is for reflection on where an individual is currently positioned regarding each of the elements mentioned in each excerpt. It provides a quick tool for intuitively considering (in that moment) where one is standing and reflecting on the choices being made on a conscious and unconscious level.

> *We are all in this life together.*
> *What uplifts one, uplifts another.*
> *What transforms one, transforms another.*
> *What awakens one, awakens another.*
> *Many synergetic working parts create a beautiful resonant whole.*
> *Imagine the possibilities of many individuals embracing their divine missions.*

This is the world I desire to inhabit and co-create for those who follow in generations to come. I know a part of you is reaching for a new level, a new understanding of yourself and your purpose in this life. You have been led here by your intuition, a willingness to trust yourself and where you are being called.

For whatever reason, the time is now, and human consciousness requires it not just for survival but for our greatest evolutionary potential. We are now working more consistently in partnership with our soul as opposed to being run by the ego. A powerful part of you has made the demand to step into your extraordinary life, not just for you, but for those you love, the collective and for life beyond our living. Choose experiences, companions and beliefs that support your destiny.

'Set your life on fire. Seek those who fan your flames.'
– Rumi

---

*Note to the reader: As with my previous books, you may like to use this part of the book as an oracle to further assist identification and clarification around your soul purposes and missions. Asking:
What do I need to know today to open more fully to my soul mission?
Which guest contributor has information for me pertaining to my soul mission?
What change in perspective will enhance connection with my soul guidance and mission?
What can I release to accelerate connection with my soul mission?

OUR DIVINE GUESTS

Marvel in the mysterious and mystical

A. A. MILNE
Author

Find the writer in you; it will soothe your soul and connect you with the creative force that guides your life.

Take care of the children in your world as they set the tone for the future that we all can't wait to see. The power of a child's imagination, combined with their 'nothing is impossible' stance and innate vibrant energy creates magic in its wake. Observing a child's foray into fantasy and creative play serves as a reminder to serious, responsible adults to let loose, drop the masks and armour, and to indulge in the feel-good, miracle-attracting nature of fun and play. Read to children, create stories with them. Encourage a love of literature and books. Teach them that books are treasured timeless gifts and contain much wonderment within. Books teach children (and adults) about life and provide opportunities for experiencing a multitude of roles and opportunities. Teach them to dream and imagine in all their days. Children contain the present and the future magic we desire to see.

A.A.'S SOUL MISSION

To write of beautiful simple moments and use the power of words to evoke fantasy, play, warmth, imagination and connection.
To lead self and others closer to the true self.
To be a vessel for creative expression.
To bring the joy of story to the world.
To establish books as enduring legacies.
To promote a love of literature within children.

Guidance for today

Be a writer. Write notes. Write letters. Write on appealing stationery. Write up recipes. Write poems. Write love notes. Write down goals, dreams and affirmations. Indulge in some journalling and automatic writing to channel the higher self to gain clarity in life. Remember the somewhat lost art of handwriting. There is great power and presence involved in picking up a pen and choosing to write ... anything.

THE CHOICE

Open up to the world of literature for learning, creating, elevating, inspiring, growing and teaching. Or ... be a closed book—closed to life.

A . H
Office Bearer

Lean into the light to make your amends powerful.

Within all of humankind there exists the potential for great light and great dark. My life serves as a reminder of the evil that can be inherent in man if the ego is left unchecked and in total domination. For me, there was no limit to the power that was craved; it required appeasement at all costs. My ego told me stories that were simply not true, but I listened, and I served all of its agendas. I was a mad man, and the very worst of deluded men as I wielded my power as a weapon of destruction. My hideous legacy still echoes throughout time and is now for the purpose of creating awareness around the great need for connecting with the light within, and for connecting with the higher self to create living that is in alignment with the new directions we require for the planet.

Check your ego; be a constant observer of your mind and its illusionary power. Negative messages and viewpoints, the need for drama, seeking control, desiring power over others, wanting to win at all costs, greed and needing to be right are ways the ego creeps into and poisons the mind, then the heart and then the life of man—and in my case, many.

Karma is a powerful record keeper. What is delivered by man is returned to man in like. Make amends your mission as required if you wish to find your peace and light. There is always hope and there is always the potential for transformation. I have much work to do in my next life. It is a big life ... bringing global transformation to absolve the darkness of my previous incarnation.

The light within me will prevail.

A.H'S SOUL MISSION

To wake up the world to the potential for destruction and heinous suffering that can originate within the mind of dark-filled, ego-dominated men. Create a global impact that can never be forgotten, so never repeated. Tread the dark path to know the dark path. Move towards the light.

Guidance for today

Learn from the dark within men throughout history. There have never been, nor will there ever be winners when war is raging within the self. Become globally intolerant of destructive expressions of the dark within humankind. There is power in collective light. Know what is going on within your own world and within the whole world. Each person who heals contributes to the healing of the world.

THE CHOICE

Avoid, at all costs, repeating the sins of the fathers.
Learn, observe, act. Extinguish the dark (with the most powerful light) wherever and however you can. Turn the past into the potential for great awakening and a desire to create a better world.

AGATHA CHRISTIE
Author

Delve into the mysteries within life.

Be a great detective in life. Be open to the mysterious, mystical, magical and unexplainable. How uninspiring if we knew it all! Wonder and curiosity create much growth and opening to potential and possibility. Always be willing to see more than what may be initially presented. Life is great at red herrings. Question, challenge, ponder and see through illusion of all kinds—both spoken and inferred. Know what you know. Trust that you always know.

Human nature is a universe of its own. No two beings are alike, and each person has shadow aspects and unpredictability. Rely on and become fully acquainted with self (first) and then you can model for others how to meet the best versions of themselves.

The more you learn about self, others and how life works, the more power you will have behind all your missions. Wisdom is power. Power fuels life.

AGATHA'S SOUL MISSION

To create.
To write.
To embrace and represent the power of imagination and mystery through writing.
To bring joy through the entertaining power of story.
To explore life.

Guidance for today

Maintain an air of mystery. The world does not need to know every aspect of you or understand all your personal truths. Keep a special part of yourself just for you. Fill it with love. Let this powerful part lead your life. Keep your creations within your heart until you are willing to birth them into the world. This approach keeps the energy that surrounds your dreams fresh and powerful as it does not become imbued with the energies and sometimes derailing opinions of others.

THE CHOICE

Understand and star in the game of life. You and your missions will benefit greatly. Embrace life as the unfolding mystery it truly is for all—personally and globally.

ALBERT EINSTEIN
Scientist, Physicist

Embrace the magic and wonder interwoven throughout life.

Curiosity, questioning and imagination make the world turn. If your thoughts are not directed towards creativity, awareness, love, growth, healing and transformation, then they have the potential to be your greatest foe. Small minds and even smaller lives arise from enslavement to senseless thought. Be the orchestra of your mind, play it well and you will create a symphony that ripples out into the world. Make beautiful music.

Your divine purposes and soul mission information arise from the quieter higher self. Bring awareness to the ego. Calm and still the ego into greater obedience to you as the being behind it. This will enhance connection with your true wisdom, essence and the guidance required to successfully navigate your way through life, for life.

Humankind requires a new manner of thinking if it is to not only survive but thrive. Thoughts are as powerful as words. Mind your mind well. Every thought has a wavelike effect, setting something of likeness in motion.

ALBERT'S SOUL MISSION

To demonstrate how the world and life works both within the seen and unseen realms.
To demonstrate the power of a strong, highly functioning mind.
To open to cosmic, infinite intelligence and to seed this on Earth.

Guidance for today

What can you see that has been previously unseen? Live from the space of 'nothing remains the same' and 'nothing is as it appears to be'. Be open to newness and discovery within all your days.

THE CHOICE

Be curious, playful and imaginative ... or stifle what you can be through control, order and by placing unnecessary significance on unimportant and limiting stances and ways of being.
Change your thinking to change your life.
Nothing new can arise until it is new within the world of your thoughts.

ANNA NICOLE SMITH
Model, Actress

Get to know a person, not an image.

Live through the soul, not the ego, to navigate your best life. Life is for living large but it also for valuing simplicity, quietness and experiencing love in all its forms. Value those who value you and let the rest go where they need to go. Do not get consumed within the world of another. Trust in your own path and personal power. Know where you dissipate your power and take action to call it back to you, for you. Face what needs to be faced in order to be healed. There is no escape from self and it is not in our best interests to do so. Learn your lessons well: grow, even transform, it will be your greatest, most rewarding work. An excess of anything is the antithesis of achieving growth and connecting with true potential. Gratitude for the smallest of things is deeply healing and grounding. Daily centring of one's being through whatever means possible should be a focus. From here, life can flow with more connectedness, integrity, love, authenticity and purpose.

ANNA'S SOUL MISSION

To explore contrast and to seek and find balance in all things.
To demonstrate the paradoxes within life to shine light on truth.
To heal and to love.

Guidance for today

We come into this world alone and depart alone. Make yourself the centre of your world to become the best you can be for yourself—and then allow your love and energy-changing ability to flow to others. All our dreams and relationships are enhanced by meeting the best version of self. Connect deeply to all that is truly important for you. Every individual knows what is true and vital for them to succeed in life. Avoid allowing anyone to captain and even steer your ship. Follow your inner compass without distraction to allow the unfolding of your best life.

THE CHOICE

Peace or excess.
Balance or chaos.
Wisdom or unconsciousness.
Higher self or ego.
Heal or atrophy.
Co-dependency or personal freedom.

ARETHA FRANKLIN
Singer, Songwriter

Connect with the freeway to love.

'I Say a Little Prayer' for you all. My prayer for you is that you seek the love within to meet your amazing soul missions and simultaneously experience and draw in all the love that you deserve along the way. Life is so much easier if you make love your ally, your intent for being. Love is your superpower. Express it well. Without inner love to draw forth the love possible from the external world, it is a half-complete life; not the full, abundant, creative life that is your birthright. Love fuels our creativity and our potential as it connects us with the magnificent source of all things. Love brings us joy and although it does not always appear that way, love can exist within all things. Make your love a beautiful contagion—never underestimate its power to transform all that feels incurable in our complex, paradoxically challenged world.

ARETHA'S SOUL MISSION

To wake up and shake up the world through music.
To raise the vibration of the planet through creative expression.
To be an activist for oppressed and under-represented peoples.
To invoke love through the power of word and song.
To liberate the divine feminine.

Guidance for today

Live exuberantly, spontaneously and largely. Be larger than what life may currently be presenting—in all that you do. The world needs an expansive you, as do you and your divine assignments.

THE CHOICE

Unlearn all points of view and conditioned responses, thus releasing all in the way of your awakening to love and inner truth. Activate your missions through the power of your love and the associated connection with divine consciousness.

AUDREY HEPBURN
Actress, Dancer, Humanitarian

Elevate self, elevate humankind.

When meeting your fellow travellers for the first time in life, treat them as if you know nothing about them (despite what you may have read, seen or heard) to stay open to meeting the magic of an individual. We learn most about ourselves through connection of all kinds, from fleeting interactions to enduring relationships. For even if you've watched another's movies, read books or articles on them, or heard anecdotes or opinions via others, you may have received little of the truth of an individual. Release preconceived ideas and meet at a soul level to encourage greater focus on what is presenting for you both to authentically experience. Meetings are then elevated and open to much mutually shared love and wisdom. So many of our interactions and their corresponding potential for new awareness and growth are diluted because we advance into situations already expecting certain qualities and corresponding experiences. In doing so, we are limiting our connection as it is often based on a mind story as opposed to true perception. We never know or understand the journey of another, despite outward appearances. Be open, kind and compassionate in all your encounters to elevate yourself, others and the world at large. Each person makes a difference. Every pebble contributes to the beauty and expansiveness of the beach.

AUDREY'S SOUL MISSION

To tell my story to inspire others to survive and then thrive.
To encourage the belief that all can rise from the ashes at any stage in life.
To create in order to entertain and bring joy.
To bring beauty to life for healing, elevation and inspiration.
To shed light on the plight of others.
To be a voice for the unheard and unseen.
To learn the power of love, joy and kindness to transform self and others.

Guidance for today

Aspire to be all that calls to you from the quiet whispers of your soul. Allow your light to emerge from the darkness, to shine brightly and to be your beacon throughout life.

THE CHOICE

Take a risk or remain stationary.

AVA GARDNER
Actress

Life is an adventure in love, best shared.

Play within your relationships. Learn all you can about yourself through your connections with others. Relationships that are tumultuous teach us about what we don't want to be and have and shine a bright light on our personal set of limitations and strengths. In contrast, more peaceful, loving relationships help to bring us home to ourselves. Both have value. The key is to know when a relationship may have served its purpose and run its course. There is much to learn and therefore many relationships to experience. As we grow and change, our partners need to grow along with us for our souls to bloom, create and open up to new opportunities and potential. After much learning about life and self, find your greatest love, friend, teacher, supporter, advocate and co-creator in life, and dream wonderful experiences into existence. Some relationships are relatively fleeting while others are eternal, existing beyond this life. Know the difference, to know the best life.

AVA'S SOUL MISSION

To explore love and relationships.
To create pleasure through entertainment.
To promote equality.
To serve by contributing to the wellbeing of others.
To explore creative gifts.
To explore and express the goddess archetype.
To understand the essence and power of beauty.

Guidance for today

Be prepared for and open to growth as an everyday occurrence. New aspects of your missions will most likely require 'more' of you and perhaps new soulmates along the way to support the person you are becoming. Enjoy the expansion and awareness that is woven into your soul missions through your relationships and life experiences.

THE CHOICE

Love well and often. There is no greater joy or teacher. Your missions thrive on love, creativity, contribution and deep connection—found greatly within the highest order relationships.

AYRTON SENNA
Race Car Driver, Philanthropist

Live a high-octane life.

Always seek to move beyond where you are. Avoid standing still for too long. Move, make waves. Give your life momentum. Where can you go and what can you do that you have previously unexplored? Chase your missions. It is futile to wait around for them until you feel ready. Readiness is overrated and very fleeting. Get behind the wheel of your life. Change course often. A rolling stone gathers no moss. All that is not in alignment with your missions needs to stay in the back seat—you can be aware of all that sits there, but 'it' never moves to the front seat with you. Only your highest intent and greatest belief gets pride of place up front with you.

Enjoy a wild ride and you will look back on life with a sense of triumph for all that you risked and all that you gained.

AYRTON'S SOUL MISSION

To live an expansive, fearless life.
To love.
To dream.
To master.
To give.
To create.
To explore capacity of self.
To meet boundaries and push them further.

Guidance for today

Find the fire within your soul. Let it awaken you to all that could be if you are willing to trust in and express your greatness. You and the world need your greatness. Seek your genius in whatever endeavours capture your interest and awaken your heart. Boredom keeps you on the fringe of your life, not front and centre where you belong.

THE CHOICE

Make your life make a difference.

BARBARA WALTERS
Journalist, Television Host

Challenge anything that exists in life that is not to your liking.

You do not have to be at the mercy of this life. Invoke your divine birthright gift: choice. Practise in small ways by reviewing the little choices you make each day that contribute to the big picture unfolding in your life. Make choices that make you feel good and are for the highest good. What choices can you make today that may gift you little moments of bliss? Do not put off your happiness for a time when (_____). Fill in your own blanks. It's time for you to be happy and fulfilled now. Take action towards that end. The way we move through life with the accompanying attitudes and approaches we demonstrate towards others (and situations) are areas where we can elevate our choices.

Make the choice to give up competition with others. This will be life-changing as you will step into a greater version of you—one that will make even better choices! Free yourself of this program, for it is inadvertently telling you that what you are being and doing is not enough when, in fact, your very survival depends on being or doing something equal to, if not better than others. It's a harmful lie that limits the connection you can have with others, and it negatively affects your confidence and self-love. Celebrate the successes and joys of others without needing to match them to your own experience. Every dog has its day. Allowing all to have their day, their time, their moment opens the doors to more possibility for you. Celebrate another vicariously to celebrate life and self in a very powerful way.

BARBARA'S SOUL MISSION

To be an advocate for women.
To promote freedom of choice and speech.
To learn about life and self.
To create awareness around the truths of life.
To promote transparency and openness.
To use power and creativity to serve the greater good.
To laugh and to live the best life.
To have fun.

Guidance for today

Life hears you. It hears your desires and it knows your limitations. It is always supporting you and guiding you forward. You are not meant to be stagnant. Your inner creative source demands that you continually grow and step into all that you planned to be when designing your life before your birth. Receive your guidance to meet what is yours to have and be. If you are willing, there is nothing you cannot release that stands in the way of you and your greatest soul missions. Open to all of yourself by establishing a great connection with your higher guiding self and universal source energy.

THE CHOICE

Co-creation is the state you need to seek for contentment and success within all your missions. Life is too challenging to navigate alone—go beyond this world and draw forth great love, wisdom and power to support the dreams that are calling to you. Change your choices. Change your reality.

BENJAMIN FRANKLIN
Founding Father of the United States, Publisher, Inventor, Innovator

Meet your genius within and be the change the world needs.

Life is a paradox. Embrace uncertainty to maintain sanity. Flow with life and, at the same time, do what you can to make the best of all encounters and experiences. Create an inner creed to support all of humankind. You have the capacity within to raise the quality of any interaction or circumstance. Be a contributor to all of life and life will gift to you in immeasurable ways. Make mistakes repeatedly until you meet your gifts and connect with the missions encoded within your soul. Your gifts are life-changing and world-changing. The world needs the gifts of the masses unwrapped and shared!

BENJAMIN'S SOUL MISSION

To pioneer change.
To inspire, to lead.
To innovate, to invent, to create.
To be a voice for freedom, reform and new thinking.
To bring greater ease to living.

Guidance for today

Ask yourself: *What is in the way of actualising my greatness and highest soul mission?*
Let all these things go. You don't need them anymore and you never did.
Make the demand: *Show me universe on a daily basis how to meet my genius within.*

THE CHOICE

Choose ease over duress. There is great power in
peace—a portal to your talents and highest attributes.
Please make the choice to be all that you came
here to be. This choice will change the world on
a grand scale.

BERT NEWTON
Media Personality

Life is for laughing and loving.

Laugh and love your way through life to ease the burden of the challenges and hardships that accompany living on Earth. Ours is a learning and evolving planet, but we must have fun along the way to be most effective in our days. Laughter also leads to stress release and a great night's sleep. Wear life lightly and to the best of one's ability, for life is a Lilliputian glimpse of eternity, such an infinitesimal drop in a very vast ocean.

Connect with your purpose, with work that brings you joy (and simultaneously serves others) to experience contentment throughout your days.

A life that lacks meaning or purpose allows weeds to form within the mind. Manage your mind well. It is too easy for a mind that isn't fed the right thoughts to become unhealthy and unsupportive of your best living. Love yourself and all of life to provide the strongest foundation for your mind to flourish. Your mind requires your best efforts. No person or 'thing' can do the work for you. You have a choice moment to moment in how you will use your mind. Use it to create great things. Potential is first reached within a powerful mind. Do not waste your gifts by wasting your mind.

Embrace humour and understand its transformative power, both individually and collectively. Those with a media platform or 'celebrity' status can change the vibration of the world by making humour and laughter a global catalyst for joy. Presence and peace are ignited by large doses of humour.

BERT'S SOUL MISSION

To uplift, heal and transform self and others through the power of entertainment, love and laughter.

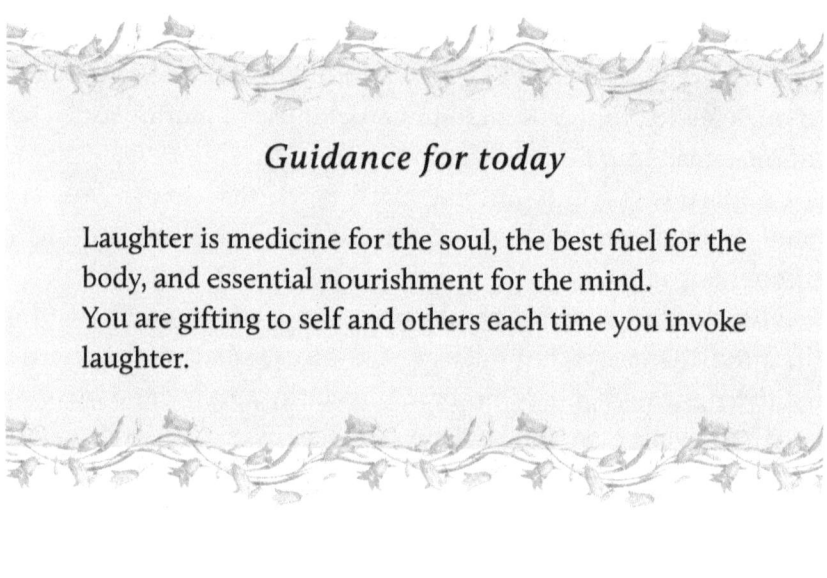

Guidance for today

Laughter is medicine for the soul, the best fuel for the body, and essential nourishment for the mind.
You are gifting to self and others each time you invoke laughter.

THE CHOICE

Activate your power, your light ... or give into limitation and less effective being. All beings can activate their own power and shine light daily in their own way where it is most needed.

BETTE DAVIS
Actress

Release the noise of the world to hear the soul.

Protect your beautiful self from the judgement that the world would have you indulge in moment to moment. Compare and despair is a toxic force spreading through many of your social media platforms. Be mindful of the collective energy that radiates around this platform. It is felt particularly harshly within us sensitive types. Protect your energy before indulging in this medium as you would before going into any particularly challenging or energetically harsh environment. Catch yourself before you fall down this rabbit hole of self-doubt-triggering comparison. It is very dark down there and makes for a challenging upward climb out. Use your social media responses to teach you about self and about all the places where you lose power to something that is not you. In fact, it is all completely outside of you. Do not be the effect of anything that is not true for you. Life is not a competition, despite this being a dominant collective energy in these times. Disconnect from collective overload and go within to find your light. Live through your heart and feel and express love as the antidote to all that hurts and wounds. Choose moment to moment to know that love and peace are your best, most loyal and comforting friends.

BETTE'S SOUL MISSION

To bring a fire to one's living and, in doing so, awaken others.
To live creatively and with intent.

To inspire women to find a voice and express authenticity.
To entertain through the arts.
To explore personal power and freedom.
To learn about honour and integrity.
To experience various human roles to learn about the self.
To learn about love.

Guidance for today

You've got this. At last, you are listening to your love and allowing it to guide your thoughts, feelings and emotions. Doesn't that feel so much better? You are meant to feel good. Life is meant to feel good. Believe it to experience it. Haven't you suffered enough and learned enough through this suffering? Give yourself permission to learn through fun, joy, love, adventure and experience.

THE CHOICE

Make the best or worst of life. It's a choice we are blessed with making, moment to moment. Look through Bette Davis's eyes and see love whenever and wherever you can. A soul mission for all is to seek and express the love the world needs.

BRIGITTE
Actress

Beauty is an opening for love, inspiration and creativity.

Receive beauty in all that is around you. Make the commitment to see and embody beauty in its myriad forms. Connect with your own version of beauty. Our individual relationship to beauty is special and unique. For one, it may be found in the petals of a flower, for others, it may be in the night sky. Commit to discovering the beauty that speaks to your soul, for within it, you will find inspiration for fuelling your dreams, desires and renewed purpose for living. Release connotations of beauty that are exclusive or artificially created. Seek the beauty within all forms of nature, wonder, awe and love.

Be the most sensual, graceful and loving version of yourself to allow others the gift of receiving your personal expression of beauty and its accompanying creativity. Evolution requires beautiful creativity. Each creative act contributes to the development of the whole.

BRIGITTE'S SOUL MISSION

To invoke the power of beauty and love.
To infuse life with goddess energy.

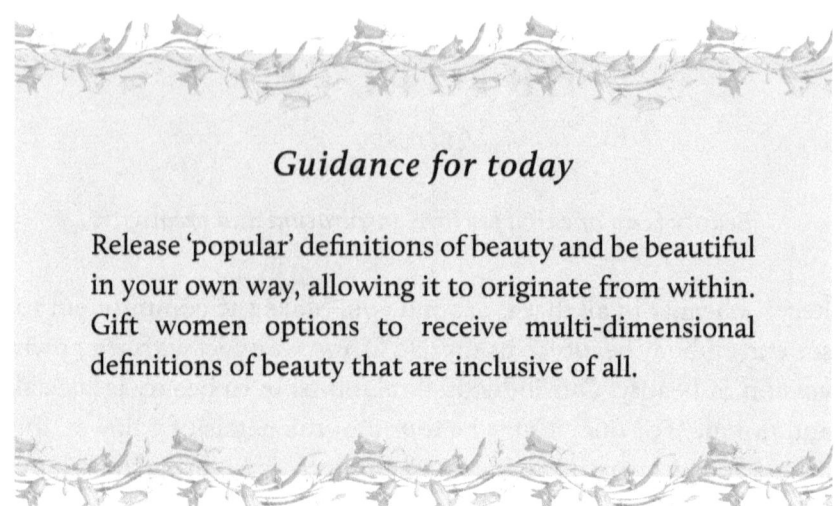

Guidance for today

Release 'popular' definitions of beauty and be beautiful in your own way, allowing it to originate from within. Gift women options to receive multi-dimensional definitions of beauty that are inclusive of all.

THE CHOICE

Embrace the beauty of the divine feminine within all things to elevate, inspire and heal. Avoid allowing your physical beauty to define or limit you. It is a mere earthly costume. Allow your beauty to evolve as you evolve in ways that best capture the true essence of you.

Author's note: Perceive the beauty around you to perceive it within. You can then allow beauty to touch all that you do and everyone that you meet.

BURT LANCASTER
Actor, Producer

Act as if life is grand, until it is.

Seek self-improvement, creativity, originality and authenticity, and you will find the 'you' required to successfully navigate your chosen missions in life. A big life awaits those who honour their missions rather than shy away from them. Your missions will not elude you or pass you by if you show up for them by simply seeking to be the best version of you. The greatest version of you draws in your greatest life, so there is no more important work than finding your inner reserves of power and then using that to serve the highest good. You deserve a grand life as you hold a very special place on Earth. Make life easy on yourself by revealing the best of you to yourself and others, no matter where it takes you or what is required of you. Life is about you (and no one else) until you get you right, and firing on all cylinders to embrace all that life presents. Don't let life take you away from connecting with and understanding your power. Life will always serve up tests, challenges and a multitude of distractions. Stay aware but also keep things light. Seriousness does not open you to the power within you. That is best awoken through love, laughter and play.

BURT'S SOUL MISSION

To create and demonstrate new potential realities through the magic of the screen.
To explore power and love.
To develop strength of mind and body.

To lead through inspiration and respect.
To embrace integrity, honour and truth.

Guidance for today

Your missions require your greatest power. Make the demand on yourself to find and utilise your power for the highest good and it will be revealed to you one day at a time in the required strength and form. Remove all substances and addictions from your life when you feel safe enough to do so. Journey back to the full strength of yourself by gradually removing all those choices you are making to dilute yourself. Do not fear your own power as it is born from love and has the expression of love at its core. Real power is built on love and is gentle, compassionate, highly aware, and is ever evolving to bring the best to any circumstance.

THE CHOICE

Choose to become acquainted with your power or risk invisibility to self and others.
Charge your energetic batteries with love and impassioned intent to achieve maximum impact within your missions.

CARL JUNG
Psychiatrist, Writer

*'Your visions will become clear only when you can look
in your own heart. Who looks outside, dreams;
who looks inside, awakes.'*
– Carl Jung

Look within your own heart and soul. Do not fear your truth. These deep truths are often revealed just for you when you need them most. Sharing your truth assists others to unlock and connect with their own truth. Do not judge yourself when your truth is not received by others—it is up to them to process what is theirs to receive in any given moment. Breathe and connect with your guidance before sharing a truth, because if you are speaking to the unconsciousness within others, the energetic backlash won't be worth your efforts. Let love lead you when communicating with others, showing you when to open or keep things within—just for you. Be mindful of slipping into ego conflicts. The desire to be right combined with unease in your body will indicate if you have momentarily combined a desire to express a truth with ego machinations. It is human nature to experience this repeatedly to create the awareness of this limiting pattern and to create the desire to be free of it. Catch it and be kind to yourself for being led there again. Compassionately forgive self. Let the reactionary feelings go, and bring your energy back to presence.

CARL'S SOUL MISSION

To guide self and others back to the true self.
To connect self and others with spiritual essence and oneness.
To create understanding of collective and individual unconsciousness and consciousness.

Guidance for today

Let all the doubts about yourself and your life slip away because they drain your strength and your true superpower: belief. These doubts are weeds and will grow if you water them. Trust in yourself and the plan for your life. Greet all that shows up on any day with love. Release your personal will to divine will to know your power and activate your mission. You do not require any validation from any source outside of you. Seeking validation or recognition takes you away from your power and moves you out of presence and away from trust. Trust is everything in receiving the daily guidance and inner desire to move you where you need to be, doing exactly what you need to be doing. As a student of life, your main task right now is to trust yourself and trust where you are being called. You are on track, on time and don't let any depleting doubts tell you otherwise. The universe has great faith in you. Bestow this upon yourself, dear one.

THE CHOICE

Make the life-changing decision to seek validation or approval only from self. Everyone is too busy seeking their own validation to worry about you, so give up the futile desire to be noticed, recognised or seen. See yourself, love yourself, and life will love you back and guide your life mission(s) in beautiful, magical ways.

CARLA ZAMPATTI
Designer

Design the life of your dreams.

Living is an adventure of the heart. The heart provides the doorway to opening to the sacred knowledge of our soul desires and accompanying missions. If it feels good, there is a considerable chance that we are being led to a potential inspired (spirit moving through us) direction or choice.

Commit to your choices with great fervency without listening to the voice of doubt. Doubt will dim you down and steal your passion and inspiration. Be your greatest champion in life and others will follow suit. You show others how to treat you and respond to you via the energy you radiate. Be your most radiant self as often and as powerfully as you can. On your non-radiant days, be extra kind and compassionate to yourself, knowing it's just a glitch and you will soon get back to the full strength of yourself. Our flat days are powerful incubation days. We are conserving our energy, going inward to connect with our intuition, ready to flourish again when the time is right. Renewal and restoration are essential to fuel our highest levels of power and creativity.

Earth life is equally challenging and wonderful. Put your best foot forward and look your finest doing it. Wearing great 'costumes' and beautiful fabrics helps us to feel good and to do good. Build fashion into your living funds. You are always worth it. Allow what you wear to become a way of cherishing yourself, expressing your creativity and inspiring others.

CARLA'S SOUL MISSION

To combine power and creativity to inspire others to reach for the wonder and healing potential of beauty and design.

Guidance for today

Creating is a fun and essential part of a fulfilling existence. Connect with what you love. Breathe life into your own form of creativity. Your creations are brought to life through love as it provides the desire, inspiration and motivation.

THE CHOICE

Create or stagnate.

CARY GRANT
Actor

Be miraculous. Your soul essence knows how. Reacquaint yourself with the magic of you. It is found in your light.

Be light and loving to bring out the best in others, and individuals can then bring out the best in you—the highest versions of self all contain a degree of reciprocity. Surrounding yourself with those who draw the greatest version of you to the forefront is conducive to light-filled, ever-evolving (for the highest good) soul missions. Your anger will trigger someone else's anger just as your laughter can trigger someone else's joy. Remember your power to enhance life all around you. Use it well. As your power and influence increase, you have even greater responsibility to use your presence for positive impact.

CARY'S SOUL MISSION

To embody light, love and grace.
To create.
To bring joy through entertainment.
To lead life by example.
To love.
To explore life and self for inner wisdom and transformation.
To recognise truth from untruth.

Guidance for today

Listen to your soul. What new direction is it desiring to lead you? You have risen above your current conditioning, karma and soul learning and are now ready for so much more. Be open to what is opening for you in life. The biggest risk in life is in not taking the risks that would expand your life into new previously unexplored frontiers. Life is truly magical and exciting if you know it and allow it to be.

THE CHOICE

Miracles, mystery and a little expansive mayhem or the mundane safety of a half-lived life.

CATHERINE OF ARAGON
Tudor Queen

There is nothing more powerful than a heart steeped in love and possibility.

You don't need constant answers or continuous success in life, despite life telling you in some form or another that these 'states' must be sought daily. Your commitment to being present will take much hard work away from you. Connect with your inner grace and it will help you to relax into your missions, allowing what is needed to flow within you and all around you, effectively responding to your desires and putting your dreams into motion.

CATHERINE'S SOUL MISSION

To question, to challenge, to express personal will and truth.
To be a voice for women.
To be a force against darkness.

Guidance for today

Relax into surrendering. Every time you relax, you allow in love. Fight or flight are steeped in fear and resistance.

Surrender personal will to divine will. Physical surrender is found in your most relaxed, calm, nurtured state. Relaxation allows the body to surrender to healing.

Surrender physically and emotionally as often as you can to function from your highest self. Release your stress to meet your true destiny and connect with the greatest potential within your life's work and overall central mission.

THE CHOICE

Do not allow your fear to stand in the way of your dreams. Life will always conspire to present you with your fears. This does not mean life is against you. The opposite is true; face what you fear enough with brave intent and love in your heart and life will help you to overcome anything—if not in this life, then beyond. There is always time by your side.

CATHERINE THE GREAT
Empress of Russia

Use your power well and be unstoppable in your approach.

Avoid being confined or defined by your birth status, race, sex or any other form of perceived label or limitation. When utilised with intent, the heart, mind and soul know no bounds. We can rise above all 'stations' in life. In fact, the more unpleasant situations we find ourselves in can provide the fire we require to rise beyond what we may (initially) have perceived as possible. Allow each small win, gain or baby step to reveal your potential, and use this to propel you forward into known and unknown directions. Life will lead you in a merry dance and create a plethora of opportunities to befall you ... if you are so willing. Be led and do your very best in whatever scenario you find yourself in. The universe rewards effort, particularly if it is connected with service, grace and love.

CATHERINE'S SOUL MISSION

To be a voice of change, reform, enlightenment and evolution.

Guidance for today

Love you to empower you. Know you are worth all that you desire and aspire to be. Embrace all that life reveals for you (without resistance) and your life will be infused with great potential. Flow with life. There is no need to fight it as it originates from a source greater than you. This guidance is a blessing. You are not alone in your Earthly missions. Take comfort in this truth.

THE CHOICE

Use your power and gifts to bring out the best in yourself and others.

CHARLIE CHAPLIN
Comic Actor, Filmmaker

Laugh well to live well.

Use your platform and your influence with purpose. Every improved life has a flow-on effect. What improves the life of one, enhances the lives of many, such is the interconnectedness of all of life. Elevate yourself first to be more successful in your endeavours to elevate others. A full cup is most powerful. Find what you love doing and turn that into paid service that contributes effortlessly to the whole. Joy and laughter are great connectors as they are universally understood and valued. Bring joy to all that you do. It is a choice that can be made day to day. Joy magnifies the potential of anything that it touches. Joy is your most powerful ally for drawing all that is good and great into your world. Seek joy as you would any other life-enhancing elixir.

CHARLIE'S SOUL MISSION

> To awaken others through the joy of presence, entertainment and laughter.

Guidance for today

Laugh to elevate yourself, transmuting lower energies within you and those around you. Ego has no power in the presence of laughter.

THE CHOICE

Laugh and express the best of you in the face of all of life and live from your highest potential ... or play the role of victim and stay in a small, unfulfilling life space.

CHRISTOPHER COLUMBUS
World Navigator, Explorer

*Live your life out of the box and your most adventurous
soul missions will find you.*

Life wants to gift to you, teach you and lead you along pathways designed perfectly for you, opening you to what your soul desires to achieve in any lifetime. Break free of needing to make yourself or your life like that of anyone else. A billion unique lives will catalyse evolution.

The collective is important, however, individualism brings creativity in unparalleled ways. Everyone working collaboratively to do and be the same can often dumb down a culture rather than fuel creativity. A balance of individuality and collaboration (when required) is desirable. Each person has encoded within their soul precious life-enhancing information, yearnings, knowledge, gifts and predispositions that can contribute greatly to the advancement and enlightenment of humankind. This deep knowing is activated through peace and connection to the still, quiet wisdom within. Alone time need not be feared as it is most often when we connect with our soul guidance and ensuing Earthly missions. Obsessive togetherness and background 'noise' can be a distraction. Relish your time with yourself and receive the wonder of your unfolding potential through quiet connection to your own guidance. Avoid allowing the distractions and demands of the world, or the individuals you connect with, to take you away from you.

CHRISTOPHER'S SOUL MISSION

To explore the unknown.
To pioneer new thinking.
To discover the secrets of our world.
To inspire open-mindedness, curiosity and a questioning of limited viewpoints.

Guidance for today

Be an explorer. Let life take you where no person has gone before, if that is your destiny. Connect with and discover all you can about yourself and your place in life. Ask often, 'What am I here for?' / 'What is the greatest plan for my life?'. Call on your higher self and divine guidance and say, 'Lead me where I need to go for the highest good.' Live your life in states of wonder for what is occurring within you and all around you in response to listening to the wisdom of you. You are like no other and are here to live like no other.

THE CHOICE

Be like everyone else or be like the greatest version of you. The world needs our unique, brave brilliance, not our conformist, safe self.

CHRISTOPHER PLUMMER
Actor

Life occurs on an ever-oscillating continuum utilising both order and chaos for growth.

All conditions experienced are important for movement in life. Disparity, discrepancy, disorder … enjoy them all. Don't be disappointed by life. Don't let it hurt you or chip away at you. The key is to remove your expectation of situations and people, then everything unexpected is a bonus or a great blessing depending on your point of view.

Unhappiness is caused by the great gap—the divide between what we 'expect' and what occurs. Bridge this gap and add greater peace to your days. Always anticipate wonderful things unfolding in your life and, at the same time, value whatever occurs.

There is a grander, more intricate plan for you, just beyond perception. Trust that what is happening is an integral part of the growth required for the highest order of yourself and your accompanying soul missions. Life isn't always pleasant; free yourself by not expecting it to be always displaying the rosy side of things. Thorns are just as important as blooms, for all aspects of any creation have purpose. Life is for growth, expansion, consciousness, contribution and love. Events and experiences to support these ends will involve nuance, complexity, timing and outcomes beyond our control—nor should they be controlled by us. While we do limitation, the universe does not. Surrender to life on life's terms. Love and appreciate all your days because what unfolds is perfectly imperfect for you.

CHRISTOPHER'S SOUL MISSION

To create.
To entertain.
To explore and express life through the arts.
To lead.
To love.
To serve.
To master and express gifts and talents, inspiring others to do the same.

Guidance for today

Learn to love the little things. From the little things, dreams, magic, love and great possibility can grow. Start small and think large, whilst owning and appreciating what occurs.

THE CHOICE

Release victimhood, regret, neediness and disappointment. Embrace gratitude, hope, optimism, wonder, love and surrender. Be in your essence and at peace with all things.

CLARK GABLE
Actor

Live multiple lives within one life.

A good life contains many chapters. It means one has opened, stretched, ventured down unknown tracks and changed trajectory often. There is too much to experience in life to find one thing and do it forever ... unless you continue to grow within said choice— and create anew throughout it. Each chapter in life brings with it new skills and an accompanying new persona. We learn to become multi-faceted. We surprise ourselves with new gifts, attributes, wisdom and abilities each time we re-invent ourselves, even if on a small scale. We are like pyramids building a strong layer on top of strong layers until we reach a peak—a peak that can continue to grow, for we are infinite. Each chapter has value, especially those that you feel have nearly broken you as these create the pressure for transformation, questioning and reviewing self and choices. An opening occurs to guidance and other previously unconsidered courses of action through duress, particularly upon peaceful reflection when a tumultuous situation has passed.

CLARK'S SOUL MISSION

>To re-invent life for self and others.
>To venture into the world of potential.
>To reach new levels of strength.
>To choose self.
>To expand from the known to the unknown.
>To love.

To forgive.
To create.
To receive and bring pleasure through the creative arts.
To learn through relationships.

Guidance for today

Explore personal talents and opportunities to more fully meet your potential, and to add new elements to enliven and enhance your soul missions. Trust that the wheel can always be re-invented even if it seems complete right now. There is always a new perspective and more creativity available.

THE CHOICE

Keep making new choices. Choose, choose again and repeat. Choice is creativity in motion.

CLEOPATRA
Egyptian Pharaoh

Beauty arises within and radiates outward. Gift yourself the power and potential of your own manner of beauty.

Beauty is our essence, the place from which we bloom for others to see and to take pleasure in. True beauty is inclusive and an invitation to be and experience what is possible in life. How will your beauty touch others? How will you invoke your own beauty? Love yourself and care for yourself relentlessly to meet the most formidable expression of your beauty.

Beauty is not meant to be competitive or invoke feelings of inadequacy or comparison—this is ego-defined beauty, not soul-originating beauty. The latter is an expression of love and potential, the former is steeped in fear and limitation. Ego-centred beauty is never satisfied. There is always fault to find and things to fix or mould into inauthentic, often unnatural expressions. Age is not to be feared as it does not steal beauty. Ego-based attitudes and fearful living weaken beauty. Beauty is never lost as long as we remain connected to the love within and all around us. Beauty is a moment-to-moment choice.

Look to nature to witness the power of beauty. Patterns in bark may be beautiful, dewdrops on leaves may be beautiful, an unfurling bud may be beautiful, tawny coloured, exquisitely textured fallen autumn leaves may be beautiful. Nature is not limited in her definition or expression of beauty and nor should we be. Flowers choose to bloom within their garden when it is their time, and they are willing to bloom often. There are many expressions of beauty within nature. There is something for everyone to love and appreciate and it does not necessarily mean full bloom all the time. No one wants to feel the pressure to bloom repeatedly. It is not natural. Beauty requires restorative, quieting times for nourishment and replenishment as witnessed in nature.

Connecting with your divinity is beautiful and will make you feel more beautiful than you can imagine. Connect with goddess energy to know your beauty.

CLEOPATRA'S SOUL MISSION

To balance power and love to transform self and others.
To meet the full extent of power arising from worth.
To bring beauty and its potential for love to self and others.
To embrace mysticism and healing to transform self and others.
To lead others towards light.
To connect heaven and Earth, bridging the gap between the two.
To release fear and experience love in all its forms.
To know the power of love and magic combined.

Guidance for today

Lead from the heart and know that your worth is your true power. All decisions, and all that we allow ourselves to receive, come from how worthy we consider ourselves to be. Work your worth as if your life depends on it, because it does.

THE CHOICE

I am worthy of all that I am and all that is destined for me.

COCO CHANEL
Fashion Designer

*Know the beauty within your soul and be beautiful
for every age of your life.*

Beauty is an internal state. It arises from our essence. It must be felt within before it can be externalised in a way that feels good. The 'costumes' you wear will be loved by you if there is love within. If not, there will never be enough costumes. The ego will demand more clothes, more procedures, more tweaks, more of everything that is draining of you, your energy, your time and your resources. Know you are enough to be enough. Be the designer of your own life and present yourself to life in ways that represent the unique essence of you. Be brave in your choices and in your fashion. Fashion is for fun and for feeling good. You deserve to feel good and look good in whatever way resonates with you and best reflects your budget and life. Your clothes should make you feel even more comfortable in your own skin. If you wear your clothes with confidence (without allowing them to wear you) as a true expression of yourself, then you will feel empowered, elegant and authentic. This is true beauty.

COCO'S SOUL MISSION

To open self and others to the power of creativity.
To invoke beauty as a means of opening to light and love.
To raise the vibration through the elevated emotions associated with design and fashion.

Guidance for today

Embrace your grace and reflect this in the 'costumes' you choose to wear. Celebrate the essence of your beautiful self by confidently putting your best foot forward. Every day you can stroll down your own catwalk.

THE CHOICE

Choose your unique form of elegance and beauty ...
or deny the true essence of you.

COLLEEN MCCULLOUGH
Author, Neuroscientist

*Embody your work to create a magnificent mark and
a true reflection of you.*

Life is a great teacher. Through a complex system of signs, symbols and synchronicity, it reveals to us any weaknesses evident for transforming into greatness on a daily basis. Over time, life also reveals to us the latent talents and abilities we possess for best creating our lives. Avoid missing your guidance, as it can be a whisper, a single moment in time. It's much easier to catch onto guidance related to healing and any necessary lessons for growth the first time around. Tests and challenges can grow in magnitude if we miss the magic in the lesson. Avoid resistance to your 'teachers' in whatever form they take. A lack of connection to our awareness creates delays in bringing our dreams into the field of our existence and can create the necessity to repeat scenarios that are not always favourable. Be a learned student in the school of life to open the gifts bestowed within you before your birth. These personal aptitudes have perfectly and imperfectly equipped you with the necessary attributes for successful soul missions. Find what moves you (within) and follow the trail these responses lay out before you. You are meant to seek happiness and experience happiness for a large portion of your living. Happiness, success, abundance and fulfilment are key ingredients of soul missions. Enjoy what is yours because it has been designed beautifully for you in the stars. You are a shooting star, blazing a beautiful trail behind you.

COLLEEN'S SOUL MISSION

To understand life: past, present and future.
To ignite light.
To create.
To learn from history, and to present it authentically.
To write in order to teach, inspire and entertain.
To explore the possibility and potential within life.
To love and heal.
To give and receive.
To create abundance.
To use soul gifts.

Guidance for today

Be a master of all that you do. Value excellence. Honouring your work is a sure-fire way to make it count, to give it life and to create a timeless legacy. Find the passion that resides within your soul and bring it to the forefront of your life. Passion is an underestimated powerful force of creation. Create away and enjoy the natural unfolding of your soul missions.

THE CHOICE

Boredom will not lead you to the pinnacle aspects of your soul purposes, paths and missions. Bring excitement, enthusiasm and spontaneity into your days. Your energy then becomes a living, breathing entity with a life force of its own. Be the force of nature that you truly can be. Let the leaves rustle in your wake.

D. H. LAWRENCE
Author

Use your talents well to create your best life.

Embrace your aloneness. With so much focus on the importance of connection, we can forget the power of solitude. It is in the quiet times, free of distractions, that we meet the power of ourselves and open the space needed to work on and create our own dreams. My books arose out of stillness as I could hear the calls of my imagination, inner wisdom and muses. Our innate gifts and talents need nourishment in the form of peaceful space to fully surface and for us to know how to utilise them for the highest purpose. It is difficult to be the best version of ourselves if we are always co-mingling with the energies, challenges and dominant attributes of others. Know yourself first before others. Self is the only life-enduring confidante we can ever fully know and rely on. We arrive on the planet individually and leave individually. We know how to 'do' alone more effortlessly than life would indicate. Find your balance between alone time and outward connection. Both are important in this life.

D. H.'S SOUL MISSION

To challenge societal norms to create greater freedom of authentic expression.
To write in order to teach and open up awareness of possibilities within life.
To create.
To love.

Guidance for today

Create some quiet space to ponder the wisdom that wishes to arise within you to enhance your soul missions.
Avoid basing your worth on how many relationships and connections you have. Being alone is always better than engaging in toxic relationships. Who we spend our time with significantly influences how we feel and in turn what we believe about ourselves and the accompanying choices we make.

THE CHOICE

Be your own best friend and many will desire to befriend you.
Being alone is a choice, even a great choice. Do not, however, be a victim of aloneness. There are always opportunities for connection, if that is what your soul desires. Stay open if you wish to draw in connection from both expected and unexpected sources. A loving heart without armour is an invitation for connection.

DIANA
Princess of Wales

Love is the only way.

I am extremely proud of my boys. Although a life of privilege has been an inherent part of their journey, there's has been a difficult path to navigate.

One has been duty 'bound' since my passing, carrying the weight of the world on his shoulders. He will find his own beautiful way of bringing much-needed change to guide and help many.

One has been aware of the harmful paradoxes within his living and continues my legacy of shining light where it has not previously shone, helping the world to 'see' what can no longer be 'unseen'.

The two who have had to separate to be harbingers of change will become whole again. Love will prevail, uniting powerful families with mutual understanding and activation of core missions as the essence. Leadership will be with and through light.

Ancestral lineages will be changed for the betterment of those who follow. Upheaval is the prelude; peace is the outcome.

DIANA'S SOUL MISSION

To heal.
To love and be light, helping those who do not have a voice.
To bring truth to the forefront of humanity.
To transform fear into love.
To shine light where there was darkness.
To find personal power.
To nurture.

Guidance for today

Remember that nothing is often as it appears to be on the surface. Many beings present half-truths with an accompanying agenda. Learn to connect with the truth in any situation via your own internal compass. Be quiet enough to connect with the power of your guidance—you can then assist the process of shifting what no longer serves the highest good of our newly evolving world; a world with greater freedom from the old paradigms of limitation, control, inequality and oppression. The dominant voices can then experience the dimmer switch, paving the way for quiet truths and life-changing wisdom and consciousness.

THE CHOICE

A blind eye does not create the vision the world so desperately needs. Turn your eyes to see the truth, even if it is confronting. There is freedom on the other side of falsity.
Lift the veil and see behind the curtain of illusion. Many opened eyes have the potential to open many great and influential minds and hearts.

DOLORES CANNON
Author, Hypnotherapist

*Life contains many gifts for those brave enough
to boldly share their own.*

Life is convoluted, so much so that it is of great benefit to understand and focus on one's own patch of land before taking on the issues of the world. Your task is to be the best version of you, and in doing so, prepare for your personal soul missions before venturing out to seek the largesse of the world. Personal missions before global missions. You will be led to global missions (if that is part of your life design) when you are activating healing within and moving through the lessons interwoven through your personal missions. Life in the world is challenging and tough for those showing up ill-prepared. Do the work on yourself first to work your magic most successfully on the world. Your magic will amplify ease and grace, and encourage you to extend greater kindness to self and provide opportunities for deep contentment.

DOLORES'S SOUL MISSION

To be a 'bridge', bringing spiritual information and understanding about how the universe works onto the planet to create awakening and consciousness.
To recover lost knowledge for the benefit of humankind.
To make connections between past, present and future lives for greater soul evolution.
To promote inner healing, leading to wholeness.

Guidance for today

When whole, expand your consciousness to connect with the oneness of the world, thus contributing to and expanding universal potential.

THE CHOICE

Show up for all of life in a way that is a unique expression of you and not influenced by any other. We need people who are leading their lives and creating anew, not following like grazing flocks of sheep. New, lush pastures are calling to those willing to venture into the unknown without a guide or plan other than the powerful guide encoded within. Be yourself, listen to yourself (and your higher self-guidance), and you will find your way most beautifully in this life.

EDGAR ALLAN POE
Author

Be the stars that can be seen from the night sky.

There is only one life that counts today, and it is the one you are currently navigating. This life is leading you towards your most starring role to date. You are prepared (even though often you feel lost) because you have been laying the groundwork for this mission for many lifetimes. Life has been gifting you the tools, knowledge and circumstances you require for a successful mission since the day you took your first breath. Have faith in the grand plan for you. Be open to it. Receive it fully. Move with it by surrendering to the best of you. Allow life to be, for what could be more perfect for you and those you impact with your inspired life choices and accompanying soul missions?

EDGAR'S SOUL MISSION

To explore the power of the written word.
To challenge the current use and styles of the written word.
To encourage depth of feeling.
To understand and plant seeds pertaining to the nature of the universe.
To entertain.

Guidance for today

Be at one with and at peace with life. Fight only the darkness within you.
Your ensuing light will be the beacon you need for self and others who are connected to you and your journey.

THE CHOICE

Receive your divine guidance for activating your soul mission. Your soul blueprint is planted within you just waiting for you to water the seeds that will form deep roots and large blooms ... when it is their time.

EDWARD MULHARE
Actor

Slow down to receive the best of you and the best of life.

Avoid confusing tiredness with relaxation. Fast-paced lives often don't allow for relaxation and, as a worst-case scenario, many individuals don't even feel tired as fight or flight is so prevalent. To be the best you can be, tune into where you are on the tired versus relaxed continuum. Allow your body to communicate tiredness to you and give in to peaceful naps or deep sleep as required. Tiredness does not need to be avoided by using caffeine and other forms of stimulation. Tiredness is part of the body's communication system and is an important part of the restorative and healing cycle. Befriend your tiredness!

We need to be calm, quiet and relaxed to tune into where our guidance is calling and to receive powerful creative urges for enhancing action within our soul missions. Fight-or-flight contributes to stress hormones, anxiety, despair and even irrational self-doubt-induced thinking which is non-supportive of bringing forth the super self to navigate soul missions. Earth and her great challenges require much of us. Support yourself in the best way possible.

Avoid confusing boredom with tiredness. Sometimes being tired means we are tired of the life we are currently creating. Lean into the truth of your tiredness and take necessary action if you are functioning from boredom or discontentment in life. If you are on track and feeling purposeful within your missions, boredom will rarely exist.

EDWARD'S SOUL MISSION

To enjoy and explore creative gifts.
To bring light through acting and entertainment.
To explore life's mysteries.
To embrace the unknown.
To be led by life.
To stand in truth and presence.
To know and express one's essence.
To bring the best of oneself to life.

Guidance for today

Create the space to receive your life.
Life flows into openness of all kinds. Busyness is not the remedy for all that ails. Do not run from you and therefore push away what is meant for you. Life, if you allow it, will always circumvent any obstacles on your path if that is for the highest good. In all scenarios, meeting the truth of you and your needs brings you into alignment with your soul voice and soul life.

THE CHOICE

Do less well to be and attract more.
In all that you do, live from the heart and speak from the heart to enhance all encounters and situations.
Make love a powerful undercurrent in the rivers of your life.

ELIZABETH TAYLOR
Actress

Find your courage and passion as there is just so much to do and so much to be.

All the work that so many of you are doing on self must be acknowledged. Celebrate each time you face a wound. The same hurts will often appear over and over in different contexts and at different stages of life until they are clear, and you are free. Relish in the peace that comes after a cleared stubborn wound. You have earned it! Each time you face and release a wound or shadow aspect (whatever term works for you), you are helping clear the same wounds in the collective. Many of your own wounds and shadow aspects are not as personal as you believe they are—you are tapping into undercurrents within the collective. Some universal wounds (that you judge yourself for still having) such as rejection issues, compare and despair tendencies, and self-doubt are flowing through humanity right now and probably do not even belong to you. Send them back to where they came from with light attached. The light on the planet is stirring shadow aspects up to be seen (rather than bypassed) and healed. Working through your stuff is healing self and the planet. Celebrate every time you open yourself up to observe an inner pattern rather than using something to numb it or force it into a box with a heavy lid on it. If this happens too often, Pandora's box will not be fun to open. Be kind to self and gentle with your nervous system by avoiding opening your own personal 'box' too much and too soon. A little (and consistent) lid opening is best and most compassionate.

ELIZABETH'S SOUL MISSION

To love.
To create.
To entertain.
To heal wounds and release shadow aspects.
To experience a myriad of female roles.
To be and express beauty.
To explore the goddess archetype.
To learn about self through relationships.
To release karmic bonds.
To use influence and serve through activism.

Guidance for today

Befriend any so called 'enemies' within, transmuting them into wise servants willing to go where you need to go, doing what you need to do, and to be in alignment with your soul missions.

THE CHOICE

Know that not everything you feel or experience is yours! If you are sensitive, this is a vital truth for you to absorb right now. Avoid turning your beautiful, light-inducing (world-changing) sensitivity against yourself. Let the awareness of the world (and the pain) flow through you, transmuting into light along the way.

You are love. Anything that is not love and peace most likely isn't yours—just your perception of energies that are around you. Simply be aware of these energies and not the effect of them. Shine your light (not your fear) on the energies you experience and alchemise them into something greater. Your soul knows the way and knows exactly what to do. Trust in your process.

*Author's note:
A healed empath or sensitive changes the vibration of a room, transmuting energies into something greater. An unhealed sensitive absorbs the energies of a room to their overwhelm and detriment. Raise your vibration through intentional healing to return you to your wholeness. You can then use your power to effect great change and open more fully to more dynamic (or new) aspects of your soul missions.

ELVIS PRESLEY
Musician, Performer, Songwriter, Actor

Cultivate open curiosity, trusting that there is always more than meets the eye for those willing to see.

Take care of yourself, body and soul, so you create the most favourable conditions for undertaking life's missions. This will allow you to fulfill your destiny and wring the most out of life.

Throughout life, all relationships and all experiences are enhanced with a clear mind and healthy body. Wellbeing is true wealth and draws like unto itself. Meet all your missions with the best of you so you can experience the full potential of yourself with the bonus accompaniment of great fun, love and abundance.

ELVIS'S SOUL MISSION

To explore personal power and love.
To uplift humanity through music and entertainment.
To follow the heart and live from the soul.
To invoke the healing, uplifting and transformative power of music.
To challenge existing paradigms and cultural norms.
To promote equality.
To promote personal sovereignty as opposed to societal authoritarianism.
To learn and activate the power of dreaming.

Guidance for today

Serve you and serve the world. There is much pain and suffering in the world. Great intent is necessary to transmute struggle, despair and hopelessness on a global level. Do your part to make others smile and laugh—there is great power in that. Be the antidote for the darkness. Be light, and love as often as you can. Grandiose acts are not a requirement. Every small deed radiates out into the world, amplifying along the way. Know your power to create change. Be the full authentic expression of you as that is what you are here to do. Your true expression opens this within others and changes realities, opening doors to change. All who are reading this work are alchemists capable of transforming much of what ails within an individual life, facilitating a carry-on effect to all who orbit each life.

THE CHOICE

Uplift humanity by uplifting yourself to make a true connection with your soul mission. Let your love lead the way. Dream your life into existence. No one else can do it for you.

ENID BLYTON
Children's Author

Have a lifetime love affair with literature.

Connect with the power of the written word to learn, grow, love and experience the joy, wonder and magic possible in life. Be childlike, always keeping fantasy, laughter and imagination alive. Gift yourself the power of an education, embracing the many non-traditional methods of education to cater for all. Literacy is a superpower that throws open the largest doors in life—one that's filled with unique and splendid opportunities and adventures. Read to children as often as you can. Foster a culture that is dominated by the love of literacy, stories and literature. An educated population is a wiser, more aware, more conscious and less malleable population. People are disempowered through a lack of literacy. Tell stories, read stories, write stories. Write your own story well in life. Words are everlasting and powerful beyond measure.

ENID'S SOUL MISSION

To bring joy.
To bring imagination alive.
To encourage fantasy.
To foster a love of surprise, possibility, magic, adventure and mystery.
To provide an antidote for fear and suffering.
To promote worldwide literacy and the power of the written word.
To encourage allowance and acceptance of all unique

expressions of an individual.
To show possible diverse gender roles beyond traditionally established norms.
To encourage children to question authority.
To encourage living with a moral code.
To open up to the unseen realms for inspiration.

Guidance for today

There is much peace, contentment and wisdom to be activated within you through the pages of a book. Allow the simple pleasures of life to be yours. Life is not meant to be a daily grind or overly serious. Make room for lightness, brightness and play in all that you do in all of your days, and you will find yourself pleasantly and passionately on purpose and on point.

THE CHOICE

Allow literature and the inherent magic
and transformative power of it to be an enduring
and loyal love. Readers are simply kinder, wiser,
happier and more present people—and therefore
most powerful.

ERNEST HEMINGWAY
Author

Life is only the tip of the iceberg.
Look to what cannot be seen in all of your days.

Life is a catalyst for personal growth or a source of great anguish if one does not heed one's internal guidance or soul lessons. Unrest presses down hard on any individual who does not confront inner wounds. Life is for releasing (often inherited) limitation, and for healing, growing and evolving as much as humanly possible in each short lifetime. Life needs to contain more urgency as there is much to release and much to achieve in a lifetime that feels vast but is, in fact, only a short trip. Make your days count. Find your worth (your power source) and use it well to enhance your world and the world at large. Our legacies linger, make yours count.

ERNEST'S SOUL MISSION

To serve.
To entertain.
To inspire.
To explore courage and perseverance against all odds.
To understand and teach about human nature and
the human experience.

Guidance for today

Unearth your truths and set them free to create a life of integrity and purpose. Make space in each day to get quiet and listen. Avoid allowing the distractions that are evident in life: addiction and other numbing tendencies, seeking approval, deferring to popular opinion and the plethora of negative influences encountered to sway you from your true course. Only allow stories where you have a starring role to play in your mind. Your mind is the vessel from which you create your life. Manage it well.

THE CHOICE

Courageously navigate your way to the other side of disappointment. Every time life disappoints in any way, despite your best efforts, have compassion for yourself and honour the vulnerability and risks that are evident within your disappointment. Show up even more fully. Rise and rise again. If you've never struggled with the possibility of failing, you may not be stretching your parameters of 'being' anywhere near enough to open your greatness. Push the boundaries of what you ever thought you were capable of ... or live a smaller (than your true potential) kind of life.

FERDINAND MAGELLAN
Explorer

This world is yours, be open to its gifts and opportunities.

There is a map for your life. This map is magical as it rearranges itself to suit your desires, karmic lessons, highest expression and soul missions. You cannot ever lose this map as it is an intrinsic part of your soul blueprint. The amazing thing is, it evolves as you do, adjusting opportunities and experiences accordingly. Your job is to sail lightly through life, not needing to anchor to anything specific. Let the number and type of anchors that you utilise change as you change, supporting every new evolution of you. Allow life to be an adventure, remembering that you always have two amazing captains with you: your higher self and your carefully chosen guidance team. Co-create the life of your dreams, enjoying expert navigation. What will you discover today?

FERDINAND'S SOUL MISSION

To begin the globalisation of Earth through exploration.
To expand horizons.
To increase knowledge of Earth, her resources and her population distributions.
To navigate life on personal terms.

Guidance for today

Explore. What part of Earth do you desire to explore? Don't just dream about it, plan it. Universal circumstances will align to support your dreams. Believe this universal law and go forth and explore. Let more of the world experience your light. Perhaps this is a soul mission pertaining to you. If you feel restless, perhaps your soul desires some exploration, some new vistas to gaze upon for inspiration, and some new cultures to expand your horizons. Humankind benefits from movement of all kinds. We are not meant to exist as stationary beings never considering new orbits. You have the DNA of ancient explorers flowing through your emotional essence. Use this to inspire the seeking of new frontiers.

THE CHOICE

Open up to more. Realise you are a citizen of the world. Come out of hiding; leave home for a time and you may just discover some inspiring and nourishing new homes.

FLORENCE HENDERSON
Actress, Singer

Receive your joy, for you are joy.

Avoid being caught up in a collective energy that encourages the belief that life involves suffering, mundane living, hardship and unfulfilled dreams as par for the course. Some beings have signed up for great duress as part of their learning and awakening process so they can learn how to heal and transform and, in doing so, show others the way. However, the universe really wants joy for its inhabitants. Even if suffering has been a part of your mission, you can now choose to grow and learn in other ways. Joy invokes love and love elevates all of life. We need more pleasure, adventure and excitement in our lives to live through love and ignite more light.

FLORENCE'S SOUL MISSION

To learn through love.
To act and sing to express soul gifts and to bring fun, pleasure and entertainment to self and others.
To explore creative gifts.
To be and receive joy.

Guidance for today

As often as you can, be a seeker of love. Love things into your reality. Fill your heart with love over the simplest of things and feel it grow. Open your heart with the power of gratitude. Gaze in wonder upon whatever occurs for you. Even experiences we deem to be negative or highly challenging contain a version of love if we are willing to see it. A loving heart is a miracle creator and one of the most powerful forces for good on this planet. Love transforms suffering into peace, joy and personal sovereignty.

THE CHOICE

Choose joy over duress.
Learn through love. Live through love.
Believe you are worthy of the most wonderful things in this life. The universe already knows this and it would like you to catch up fast.
Be the change the collective needs by seeking your joy rather than choosing to focus on your perceived suffering. Change can also arise from the safety of joy, not just from the cracking open to the light that suffering can bring.

FLORENCE NIGHTINGALE
Founder of Modern Nursing

Be your own 'lady with a lamp'.

Use your greatest power this lifetime—your ever-growing light—to enhance life for self and others. Many of you are just beginning to feel into what it means to stand in your light and use it to create beautiful things in life. When you are filled with your light, you will feel loved, worthy, peaceful, ever-hopeful and perhaps even confidently (but humbly) powerful. Your light is magnetic to more light, and soon your days will be filled with more blessings than you can count. Share your blessings. The world needs the light of all. Each individual that recognises and utilises their light becomes a beacon for others as light is beautifully contagious. Allow it to go viral.

FLORENCE'S SOUL MISSION

To bring awareness of optimal practises to support healing.
To foster the preservation of life even in extenuating circumstances.
To serve by spreading hope, warmth and love.
To activate the light within and consequently ignite this within others.

Guidance for today

Where once all roads led to Rome, nowadays it is my hope that they all lead to wholeness. All emerging wounds are to be seen, to be acknowledged and to be healed. Do not resist what is rising within to be witnessed by your light. Know also that when you are at your most peaceful and perhaps even living your best life, things will rise from the depths of any darkness to be healed. When body and soul feel most safe, the greatest healing often takes place. Many confuse discomfort, unease and anxiety as something being intrinsically wrong, however, this state is especially right and very rife for growth. Allow your discomfort to connect you with the inner wisdom needed to guide you back to yourself. Do not be afraid of the archaeological dig. Your soul knows when it is ready to explore and find the treasures hidden under the psychological debris. Personal healing is the primary focus right now. Healed beings become healers as their wholeness allows them the wisdom and fortitude to serve.

THE CHOICE

Be a light for the world by first igniting it within. Living in the light is your personal invitation to walk through the gates of your own heaven. Open your beautiful heart space and receive the light that wishes to come to you.

FLORENCE SCOVEL SHINN
Inspirational Author

Wear life loosely, but with intent.

Life exists through divine design. A life lived without divine connection is only a half-lived life, for it is without the source and substance to make it truly great, even phenomenal.

Life isn't meant to be so hard, so challenging. We make it so via our thoughts, emotions and ego responses—which never need to reach critical detriment if we stay close to our divine source. Accessing our divinity (our true nature) softens life, expedites our karma and aligns us with our soul missions.

Ego entrapment and a consequent inability to perceive and release our shadow aspects is the Earthly junk (Earthly limitations) that we need to clear out. This spiritual de-cluttering opens us to the power of source and the power within. Your words and actions are then resonant with your dreams and desires. Inspiration can now find the space to flow in and ultimately guide you along the path of your greatest destiny. Alignment with your heavenly persona is most powerful ... you can become the force of nature that you already sense is within you, awaiting you.

Please know that there is so very much more to you than you have currently encountered. My prayer for all readers is that you meet the exquisite divine expression that you truly are. Keep showing up for the work. Go inward, reflect, transmute your suffering into something greater and prepare to meet the elevated you and your associated creative and expansive life. Awaken to the truth of yourself and you will witness the truth and potential within all of life.

FLORENCE'S SOUL MISSION

To use words to teach, transform, awaken, uplift and inspire, thus creating a lifelong legacy of possibility and evolving potential within humankind.

Guidance for today

Make the demand to set yourself free to be all you can be. Be still, be quiet and listen to the guidance that flows through, just for you. Know you are never alone. Many powerful beings walk by your side and support and appreciate all the work you do to heal yourself and thus contribute to the healing needed within the world.

THE CHOICE

Life is a merry-go-round. Be merry as you go around. Lighten up to assist the release of all that is in the way of your best living.

FRANK SINATRA
Actor, Singer, Producer

Rise above the triggers, then go beyond ...

Life will always gift you challenges that are designed to move you closer to your best self and best life. Your choice is in how you respond. Your choices enhance or lessen life. Own your triggers and your reactions, then seek to outdo, outsmart and overcome them. Do the opposite of what your trigger is demanding of you in that moment. If something creates jealousy, praise the person who 'made' you jealous—you then win over the jealousy as you've chosen empowerment. If someone brings you to anger (your choice) forgive them and you, choosing to see things from all perspectives. If something scares you, and at the same time holds an element of awe for you, do it anyway, thus putting on notice the very thing that is challenging you to stay small. If something makes you want to hide, show up even more. If you feel rejected, include yourself in something greater, creating your own personally appealing invitation. You may not be in charge of your reactions and the things that trigger you, but the response can be your own. Always sit with and breathe into a reaction and then do the opposite of what the initial response demands. Over time you will understand, own and release your response to familiar triggers. You will be free to be your best selves, my friends. Your missions will flow with much greater ease and be interspersed with joy.

FRANK'S SOUL MISSION

To allow life to unfold as an adventure.
To explore the genius within.
To love.
To create.
To inspire.
To lead.
To have fun.

Guidance for today

You are a multi-talented being—enjoy an accompanying multi-faceted life. Stretch in all directions. You don't ever have to 'be or do' just one thing. Let each 'thing' have its own paths to follow. Let your life be a maze of great potential. Get lost sometimes, try new avenues—all pathways will lead to more of the potential of you. Allow the mystery of you to unfold throughout all of your days. Life is one great, big, fun adventurous ride if you allow it to be.

THE CHOICE

Buckle up and advance along new roads. Occasionally freefall. Take calculated risks to discover what this life has in mind for you. Enjoy the grand design for your life. Find your own 'rat pack' to adventure through life with. Fun shared is fun amplified. Collaborate with like-minded, inspiring souls. Talents shared flourish and can even morph into something totally unforeseen and revelatory. You are creation in motion.

FRANK ZAPPA
Musician

Freedom is a state of mind best served globally.

When choosing to conform or live in fear, one can be controlled. Instead, express individuality and personal truth to live the life planned for you, expertly designed in spirit. You do not need to know or understand your soul mission as it unfolds for the highest good when both circumstances and your current state of being are aligned. Often, you will be given a push which may be gentle or life-altering according to how far off course you may be tempted to veer. The universe's specialty is course correction. Rest assured life will orchestrate itself to support the mission you co-created before your birth. Listen to the whispers and respond to the nudges along the way. The whole picture is never revealed as the plan continues to morph itself to suit where you are at and where you have the capacity to go. As you evolve, your mission will often evolve concurrently. Perhaps you have 'outgrown' your original mission—such is the amazing nature of what you have accomplished. Your potential and therefore your mission is unlimited. Keep expanding and opening to where you are called.

FRANK'S SOUL MISSION

To explore and advocate for freedom.
To awaken new thought via creativity and music.
To challenge and question the status quo.
To bring awareness to the limitations of conformity.
To be, receive and gift love.
To overcome fear and its derivatives.

Guidance for today

Say yes to your mission and where it desires to take you. Resistance causes malaise, stagnation and even illness if we use fear to block our trajectory. Sit quietly with all forms of resistance to seek the truth underneath it. Are you being called to stop, slow down, re-route or surge forward? The answers are within your heart space. Connect to this guiding force daily, hourly. Become a living question, always seeking more of your truth and guidance.

THE CHOICE

Break free to be all you came here to be. Let love lead the way, for it is the only truly successful, peaceful and joy-producing modus operandi.

FRANKLIN D. ROOSEVELT
American President

'The only thing we have to fear is fear itself.'
– Franklin D. Roosevelt

Life is a miracle. Holding this belief will transform much if it occurs on a global scale. Miracles arise when the power of the heart fuels the mind. We need many hearts ignited by light to transform much of what ails in modern times. This message is not new, but it is more necessary now than ever. Planet Earth has arrived at many pinnacle crossroads in time. If you are reading this book, you are seeking the road less travelled for the betterment of all. Humankind is currently seeking all manner of miracles even if this is not readily identified due to the distractions of war, crime, oppression, disaster, disease and poverty issues garnering much attention. Millions of desires (prayers) are rippling around the world and changing Earth's frequency—such is their power. Keep your dreams alive, as there is much power in this. Dreaming is never wasted because it elevates the soul, stretches the mind in productive ways and connects with many other dreams occurring simultaneously throughout the world. Resonance amplifies potential. Keep seeking and radiating the power of you, your visions and your energy out into the world. You are more powerful than you can perceive at this time. Keep reaching for more and the world will reach with you.

FRANKLIN'S SOUL MISSION

To lead new belief and new life.
To create states of freedom.

To explore the potential within life.
To provide a voice for the oppressed.

Guidance for today

Release your fears lock, stock and barrel before they consume your life force. Much of what you fear is based on a hologram of a conditioned past, where certain thoughts and viewpoints have been dominant for so long they have become ingrained in cultures and infiltrated the collective psyche. Know what is not yours to keep. Only love is real. When you veer away from the path of love, you will feel unease (at the very least) or fear bordering on terror (as the extreme). Use your fear as the call, the motivation, to return to love. Do this through whatever means work for you: nature, writing, prayer, movement, creative expression, meditation, self-care and all the plethora of healing modalities, books and guidance that call to your soul.

THE CHOICE

Remember you are free. Freedom is a powerful creative force when combined with love, light and the intention to serve. Great, heart-inspired service has the potential to transform all forms of darkness into light.

FREDDIE MERCURY
Musician

Be a champion in this life.

Mercury is rising. Be encouraged by knowing that all is well beyond this life, even more so when there is a life well-lived before leaving this life and travelling to the great beyond. Life reviews are even more amazing when personal soul contracts and missions are achieved and honoured. Life and the afterlife are both spectacular, each serving different purposes. The key is to bring one's heavenly persona onto Earth, living from love and truth and in the space of openness and reflection. Be curious about all that you are and all that you experience. Be inquisitive and learn to see, hear and feel. Avoid responding to overwhelm with numbing tendencies—nothing that you are here to learn can be buried for long. There is too much treasure to uncover. Earth is a complex and challenging planet. Learn to settle into the chaos as much as the joy. Both are equally important in allowing you to face the worst of you to meet the best of you. Be a great student in your school of life. The amazing thing is … the curriculum is tailored perfectly for each of us. I have paid my dues and now I have the gift of awareness around my choices, actions and the contributions I made to the life I lived. We are works-in-progress. Each of us is an essential cog in the great wheel of life. We come from the stars and we are all stars. It is your choice how brightly you choose to shine.

FREDDIE'S SOUL MISSION

To draw down into the depths of my being to explore the full spectrum of my gifts, strengths and weaknesses.

To share the greatest of me with the world to inspire light and transformation in others.
To share my shadow aspects to create awareness in others.
To be polarising to encourage recognition of the plethora of choices and beingness in life.

Guidance for today

Breathe, people. Open up to the truth of you and to all of life. Slow down enough to perceive with all your senses. Receive all the wisdom and abundance that is meant for you. Choose heart space over head space as often as you can and then the two will work together in sync—in a musical harmony. Enjoy the complex symphony of life, appreciating the wonder and possibility of it all.

THE CHOICE

Show up for it all ... or hide away. Break a lot of personally imposed rules to meet your magic.

GENGHIS KHAN
Emperor of the Mongol Empire

Be the light within your ancestral line: past, present and future are connected and transforming much together.

Create a dynasty based on awareness, integrity, honour, love and purpose. These states endure and are passed through ancestral lines and infused within soul families. You have a great part to play in the whole, even on the days when you decide your actions are inconsequential. Nothing you do, say or choose is in isolation. There are great ripple effects. Ripple well. Be the change the generation to come needs most.

GENGHIS'S SOUL MISSION

To lead.
To explore.
To challenge.
To be great.

Guidance for today

Wherever you live now and whatever you do (in this location) is what your soul evolution and accompanying missions currently require. Do not resist. Surrender and simultaneously open up to more possibility and potential. Be in this 'now' space well—performing all required roles to the best of your ability. Do this honourably and you will naturally move onto the next stage and the next, where each is greater than the previous 'incarnation'.

Catch yourself when you move into a place of complaining as complaining only brings more to complain about and limits the favourable trajectory of any new paths that are lining up for the next stage of your journey.

········· **THE CHOICE** ·········

Be your own version of great. There is
no other choice.

··

GRACE KELLY
Princess of Monaco, Actress

Everyone has a prince or princess within them just waiting to arise.

Beauty is a much misunderstood phenomenon. Unfortunately, it has connotations of judgement, inadequacy, competition, comparison, privilege, illusion, falsity and separation. Let's release all darkness around beauty and just allow it to be what it truly is: an expression of love, a doorway to elevated feelings and a joyful life expression. Choose to look through your celestial eyes and see beauty within all things and all situations as often as possible. Be beautiful in thought, word, deed and action, and watch as life conspires to draw a wealth of beauty into your life.

GRACE'S SOUL MISSION

To be light.
To be love.
To be grace.
To inspire.
To lead beings to the light.
To be and express beauty.
To create and develop the arts.
To enhance the wellbeing of children.
To inspire women to dream and be more.

Guidance for today

Grace is an indelible quality that arises when much of what is in the way of our light is shifted back to the void where it belongs. Grace is a way of living where all that we do and all that we are is infused with love and the quiet, confident truth of us. Grace is knowing we belong, that we have a valuable part to play in life, for life. Grace insists that we are composed, we are sure. We are always enough in all situations. No being is greater than us, or less than us, just at various stages of awakening, wisdom and power. Those of us who are more awakened have more responsibility. With increasing power and increasing awareness comes more requirements and more service for the enhancement of all of life, beginning at the self-level. Self is the base of the pyramid; strong foundations are paramount. Tend to your 'self' vigilantly and ease into the potential of all your missions.

THE CHOICE

Capitulate to the light. See light within all things, within all beings, even (and especially) when they cannot see it or reach for it within themselves. Hold a mirror to another's light and increase your own light with your magnanimous way of being and seeing.

GREGORY PECK
Actor

Let your ideas and dreams be absurd, even outrageous.

Nothing truly extraordinary in life arises from the familiar and mundane. Extend the parameters of your belief in self and life to expand the possibility within your soul missions. Your missions are co-written with spirit but are not static. If you are open to unimaginable possibility, then so too are your missions in life. Infuse your life with wonder and awe as often as you can to open portals of possibility.

GREGORY'S SOUL MISSION

To push (then) current boundaries of possibility.
To embrace humanitarianism.
To dream, envision and transform new experiences into reality.
To entertain others through the acting platform.
To love.

Guidance for today

Know that magical miracles are real. What can you change within you and in current life practices to make miraculous occurrences commonplace within your life? Ask questions of your higher self and receive your personal life-enhancing guidance. It knows, you know. The keys to opening new doorways are within you.

THE CHOICE

Be open and curious to new possibilities however 'out there' and 'over the top' things may initially seem. Birth your ideas without influence from others who may not hold your vision or possess the inner fire power that you have for manifesting desire into reality.

HARPER LEE
Author

Bridge the gap between the light and dark worlds that exist within your own living.

Solidarity amongst people is most needed right now. There is great power in resonance. Amplifying great intent is life-changing and world-changing. Uniting over common beliefs and thus leading to positive movements for enhancing conditions on planet Earth is idyllic. With commitment and awareness, it is possible for us to move into living in the light on a grand scale. Your soul missions all contribute in some way to this end. You may be called to take care of things within your personal sphere, or you may have a calling regarding something on a larger scale. All missions are important as they contribute to the whole in a unique, purposeful way for your personal and world growth. Nothing is random, there is divine design in all things. Embrace and take comfort in this truth.

HARPER'S SOUL MISSION

To write for entertainment and education of self and others.
To promote a love of literature.
To bring awareness to inequality.
To explore freedom of speech in writing.
To know self.
To understand how life works and to work with it rather than against it.
To balance introversion with contribution and service.

Guidance for today

Unfortunately, in life, there are people who are willing to hurt us, wish us harm or just simply annoy us. Be aware at all times of what is occurring around you—not from a place of fear but from a place of knowing how to make the best of a situation. The world always needs our best, particularly when some individuals around us are expressing their worst. Open your intuition to support yourself in making conscious choices and acting in accordance with what transforms rather than limits situations and individuals. Navigating people can be one of the biggest challenges in life but also one of the greatest teachers. For those who you encounter (but don't particularly like), wish them well, even if you subconsciously don't wish for them much at all. Intent means something and can elevate situations of its own volition. Our collective connection means that what we wish for in relation to another, we are also inadvertently wishing for ourselves. Wish well, consciously and powerfully to be a force for positive change for self and others.

THE CHOICE

Make the choice to be a catalyst for goodness within self and others.
Claim your gifts and inherent contribution as a light worker.

HEATH LEDGER
Actor

Let your love lead you back to your inner wellness.

We prepare for life before we come to this life. We have everything we require for a successful mission. The key is to connect in regularly with this mission through the daily establishment of a soul connection, and a divine connection. Earth life has many potential distractions and attractions that can lead us away from our core truth and core missions. Become a walking prayer; be very intentional in what you allow into your mind and into your life. We are the only ones who can derail our life or allow it to veer off course. Choice is everything, moment to moment. What will you choose in the next ten seconds and in the ten after that and so on and so on? Universal laws allow us to have all that we desire. We just need to understand how life works best and do what is required to co-create best living. A great place to start is by listening to the wisdom of the higher self rather than the dramatizing, negative, limiting, ego influence that wants to make us the problem in everything ... leading us to make decisions that affect our very survival. We are not the problem. An ego-dominated and therefore unwell mind is the problem. The best life is found in moving away from the rambling mind into the observer role of the mind. Peace and power for creating a phenomenal life are found beyond the mind. Seek your peace, my friends—wherever you may find it.

HEATH'S SOUL MISSION

To overcome the mind.
To entertain to bring joy.
To learn about fear (ego) and love (higher self).
To be inspired.
To create.
To experience peace.

Guidance for today

Live your best, most content, most peaceful life today. Take a step to free yourself to be all that you can be every day. For today, just sit quietly in nature, breathe and listen. Allow nature to teach you, to show you the way. She's as good as any therapy. Allow nature to be a form of therapy. Support any therapy undertaken by finding ways to go within to connect with the heart and wisdom of you.

You have great strength and awareness regarding your needs. Don't let anyone tell you otherwise. You came from the stars; you are a star. Remember that who you really are is much more than you think you are. Meet the greatness of yourself this lifetime no matter what it takes. Make this game-changing, life-changing demand on yourself.

Choose friends, support and awareness over self-medication. Drugs will steal your essence, consume your life and eventually take your life. Drugging yourself is never the answer (unless for a specific health issue where there is no other option), no matter what you are led to believe. Be your own authority. Educate yourself about you—and about life and how it works best. There is so much information and transformative energy flooding the planet right now, connect with this frequency. Raise your vibration to become a perfect match with the frequency of the heavens and with the best of what Earth has to offer. Allow your days (and nights) to be your version of incredible. You were born for this.

THE CHOICE

Be guided by your higher self. Come to know if you are being led by the ego (mean voice) or higher self (supportive, loving, encouraging, inspirational, positive voice).

HIAWATHA
Native American Leader

Peace above all else.

Until peace is reached within an individual, potential remains unrealised. Peace is vital for power to be utilised for enhancing living. Harmony within creates harmonious experiences in the external world. All leaders should seek to generate peace within and teach those they inspire to do the same. A peaceful individual leads to a peaceful relationship. A peaceful group leads to a peaceful organisation. A peaceful community leads to a peaceful town. Peaceful cities lead to peaceful countries. Peace is the power that is so desperately needed to transmute fear, pain and suffering. Peace is far-reaching and sublimely powerful when it is valued and deliberately sought. Peace is interwoven with love and all that is great in life.

HIAWATHA'S SOUL MISSION

To activate peace within and in those encountered throughout life.
To lead by example, demonstrating the power and value of peace.

Guidance for today

Watch yourself vigilantly to ward off disturbances before they infiltrate your peaceful soul. If you are not feeling peace, look deeply within. Seek out what is underneath your unrest so you have the possibility of alchemising this condition, position or attribute back to peace. Identify the untruth—that you have perceived as real—that is leading to your anxiousness, fear, resentment, bitterness or envy. Peace struggles to exist alongside these limiting states.

THE CHOICE

Peace or darkness.
Turmoil or calm.
Success or failure.
Love or fear.
Collaboration or competition.

HORATIO NELSON
Navy Admiral

Onwards and upwards fellow beings.

Approach life with a sense of duty, for you have a duty to serve self and others. This life is not just for you. You are a great cog in an extremely intricate machine. All beings have the potential for greatness encoded within them. Unfortunately, circumstance, health and the challenges of living can derail even the best of intent. Support your fellow man or woman as each has large battles to wage within the self before great destiny can present itself—often destinies that benefit all. For many beings (who do not find their way out from under their own limitations), life does not feel enriching or purposeful. Shine light on darkness, misinformation and lack of consciousness whenever possible.

Meaning in life cannot be found until you connect with the depths of your own wisdom. Help another and you help yourself. Kindness, combined with awareness, is a personal reward and a transformative force in and of itself.

HORATIO'S SOUL MISSION

To learn about and practise honour, loyalty, service and bravery.

Guidance for today

Be willing to lead, take risks and discover that which has not been discovered before. Life is large and unlimited and needs to be lived that way. Living is a drop in the ocean of time; travel as many waters and experience all that is on offer for you. The more you open to possibility, the more possibility will conspire to lead you to great things in life.

THE CHOICE

Seek and you shall find.

HUMPHREY BOGART
Actor

Make your wellbeing the centre of your world to best show up for the world.

Take the greatest care of the vehicle that carries your soul. Positive action on the health front facilitates the best conditions for enduring soul mission work. The youth need to know that their bodies aren't indestructible and that choices today are impacting health (or a lack of it) later in life.

Many of us don't fully rise to meet the full depth of our missions until our later years. Wellbeing directly impacts the potential potency of what we desire to accomplish. Poor health weakens our life-force and the inspiration, motivation and awareness that we can connect with for embracing the full design of our lives. Take care of your physical world as you would your emotional world—both are critical and work together. The healthier the mind, the less need arises for addictive food, drug and alcohol use. Teach the youth to understand the workings of their mind and to take responsibility for their emotional wellbeing very early in life. Otherwise, they will reach for numbing scenarios as a barrier for feeling their inner world. Inner hurts must be healed before they become cavernous wounds that become too overwhelming to face.

HUMPHREY'S SOUL MISSION

To create.
To love.
To heal.

To positively influence humanity.
To embrace dark and light to learn and evolve.
To bring joy through acting and entertainment.

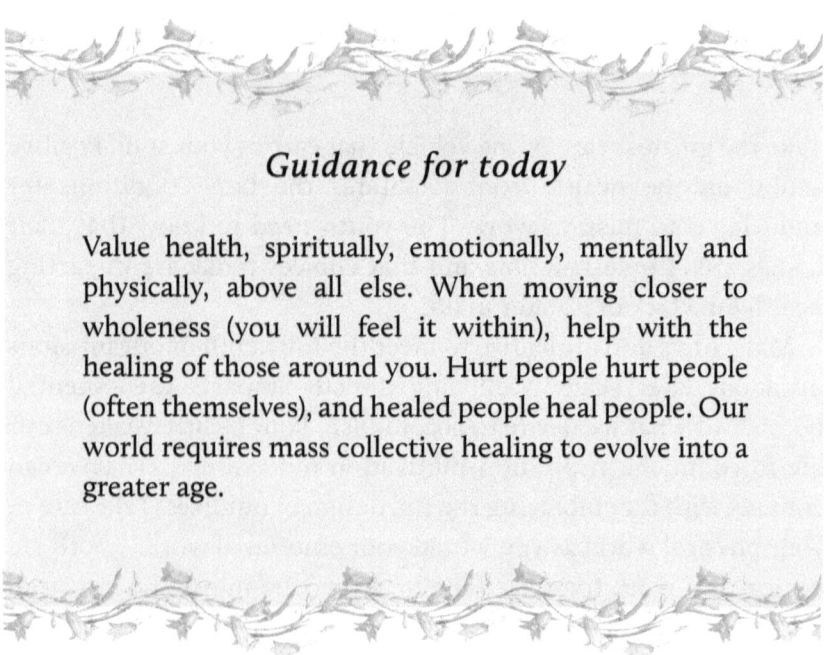

Guidance for today

Value health, spiritually, emotionally, mentally and physically, above all else. When moving closer to wholeness (you will feel it within), help with the healing of those around you. Hurt people hurt people (often themselves), and healed people heal people. Our world requires mass collective healing to evolve into a greater age.

THE CHOICE

Heal … or hinder your soul mission.
Live with no regrets and engage one's full potential.

ISAAC NEWTON
Mathematician, Alchemist, Physicist, Astronomer, Author

'For every action, there is an equal and opposite reaction.'
– Isaac Newton
Make yours count.

Understand how life works. Become a master of the game of life. You are not weak or malleable unless you avoid unlocking the wisdom within you that was encoded before your birth. Know your place on Earth and seek to expand this position as a daily intent. Heal yourself and trust yourself enough to receive your own deep wisdom. Your wisdom is found under all your stuff and accessed via a quiet mind and the peace induced by simplicity. Know your worth to issue an invitation to your wisdom. Without self-worth, you will not feel deserving enough to receive your wisdom and its accompanying possibility. You are a treasure trove of great potential, but you often insist on keeping the lid tightly closed as you fear the power of the greatness within. Do not be afraid, for your greatness is your birthright and you know how to navigate it. Look to the stars, they are not afraid to shine and nor should you be.

Appreciate that nothing is static. Anything can change anytime, and all is possible. The power of the human mind knows no bounds. However, it is bound tightly by negative and limited thinking. Words of wisdom should be valued as exquisite pearls, as portals for more, for everyone. Always seek, always pose new questions. Without questions, there is no opening to universal wisdom. Questions in and of themselves are extremely powerful. People who question are the harbingers of change, and they often don't realise that their questions are the catalysts for chain reactions across the universe. Questions and curiosity, combined with imagination invokes creation of magnitude.

Knowledge is power. Power enables transformation. Wisdom is infinite and ever evolving. The wise own the earth; take your place. Embrace the potential of the kingdom you inhabit.

ISAAC'S SOUL MISSION

To bring scientific principles and cosmic knowledge to the world for promoting understanding and enhancement of life.

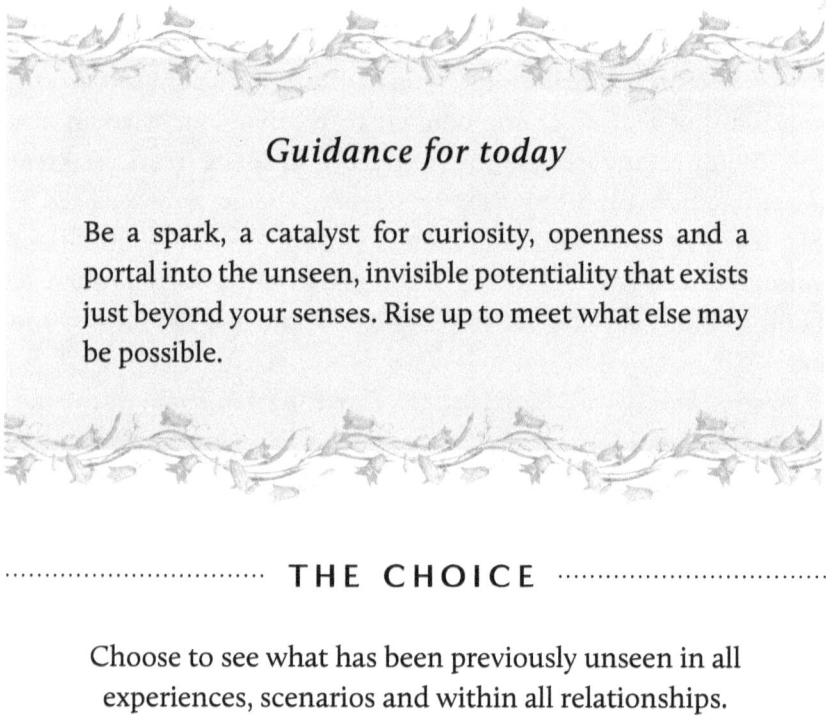

Guidance for today

Be a spark, a catalyst for curiosity, openness and a portal into the unseen, invisible potentiality that exists just beyond your senses. Rise up to meet what else may be possible.

THE CHOICE

Choose to see what has been previously unseen in all experiences, scenarios and within all relationships.

J. R. R. TOLKIEN
Author

Make fantasy the new reality.

What if fantasy is how we could create new living? Earth living requires us to stretch our visioning to create new capacities and archetypes for the next Earth chapter. The current chapter has been read for too long. We need a new, expansive prospectus. It is time for greater twists and turns, with plots that are more exciting, adventurous, magical and joyful. The old ways are no longer serving the highest expression of humanity.

Imagine a greater world into being. We are a global people. It is time to use our power to create globally.

Align dear Earth beings with the transformative alchemy that is possible with mass movements in consciousness. There is much power in collective awakening. How can you use your influence, your actions and words to accelerate consciousness for self and others? You are all great cogs in the wheel of life. Turn and turn some more.

J. R. R.'S SOUL MISSION

To invoke the power of fantasy to enliven oneself and others.
To open the imagination to more.
To utilise the power of the word to entertain, awaken, inspire, uplift and transform.
To open beings to the possibility of other worlds, other existences.

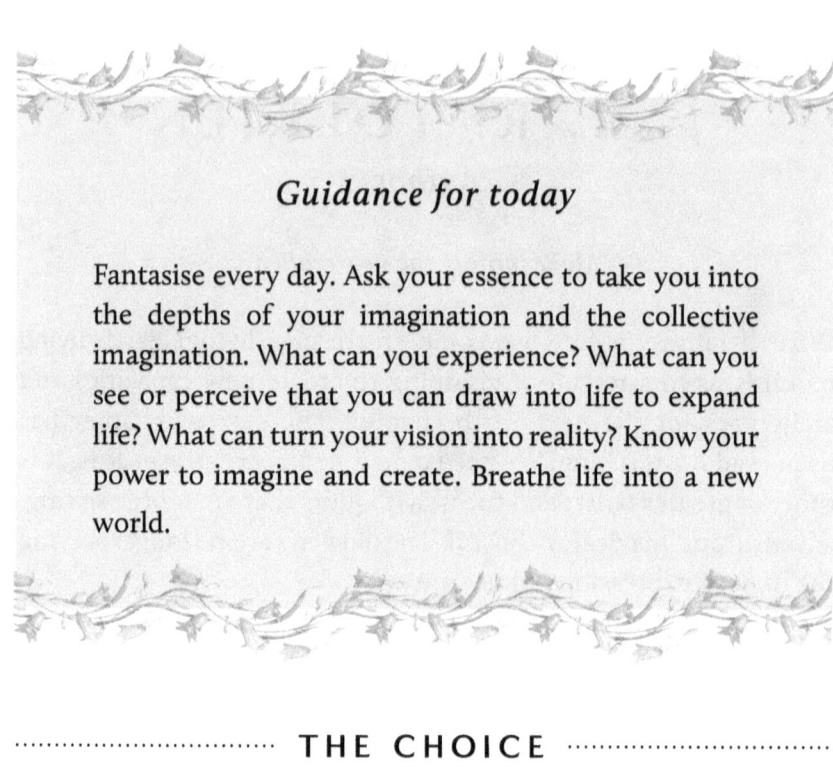

Guidance for today

Fantasise every day. Ask your essence to take you into the depths of your imagination and the collective imagination. What can you experience? What can you see or perceive that you can draw into life to expand life? What can turn your vision into reality? Know your power to imagine and create. Breathe life into a new world.

THE CHOICE

Imagine or atrophy.

JAMES DEAN
Actor

The good life arises within and is best served with authenticity.

Focus on what is occurring within you as the foundation for creating your days. Attempting to be like, or to have what another has, robs you of your own unique (and very powerful) expression. Choosing to 'not be you', out of fear or by a desire to fit in or play small, weakens the impact you can have on life. Life has a constant desire for growth, creativity and expansion, and you are an integral part of this dynamic system.

There are billions of unique sparks of light on this planet and there is a place for all. Support the movement of allowing all beings to establish the conditions required to best serve life.

The greatest legacy you leave behind is energetic in nature, encapsulating the essence of you. At the same time, you can also have a meteoric impact on life, shaking up stagnant, outdated beliefs and lineage conditioning, if you will free your soul and let it soar. Meet the real you underneath the false you and carve out deep, enduring patterns in grand canyons. Change the landscape, making it more spectacular for those that follow in your footsteps. Your steps are giant in nature, more than you can currently see through your Earth eyes. From my vantage point, however, there is evidence of magnificence wherever you tread.

JAMES'S SOUL MISSION

To assist in the healing of fractured beings.
To bring awareness and new possibility to young men.

To express the power of love and vulnerability.
To assist people in moving towards creativity and peace.
To know self for healing self.
To embody truth and authenticity.
To create and teach through the arts.

Guidance for today

Ride like the wind.
Roll with the waves.
Allow nature to provide you with great analogies for living and being. Nature heals, opens, awakens and transforms at a deep cellular level.

THE CHOICE

City dwellers, find your nature. Be in nature. Be of nature. Don't just allow all the country folk to enjoy all the peace and associated power to connect with Earth magick. Nature infuses us with the information we require to open to our soul callings and deep knowing. Bring the essence of nature into your days to meet the clearest, most centred version of you. Ground your problems into Earth and, in doing so, rise up to meet the heavens.

JANE AUSTEN
Novelist

Embrace life with equal measures of reverence, awareness and light-heartedness.

Life is an adventure for discovering one's own spirit.
Where does playfulness reside? Where does love reside?

To answer these vital life questions and connect with these beautiful states, one must follow where life leads without resistance or reaction to what is occurring. Life is not just a school room but also a playground for those who choose to approach the game of life lightly, reverently and with a desire to unlock the wisdom within. See and be seen. Freedom to be the truest expression of oneself is such a gift, one that all can receive in their own way and time whilst working within the parameters of a current circumstance or existence. Freedom begins within the mind. A clear, healthy, coherently working with the heart, style of mind is essential for great living. Manage your mind to march to the beat of your own drum—one that is most resonant with you.

Question and reflect on what is occurring both within you and around you. Often, life is ostensible, illusionary. Only you know what is true for you. Explore life via your own truths and desires. After all, it is your life, something we often forget because we are too easily influenced by, or absorbed with, what occurs around us. Awake and aware beings receive the gifts of life ... if and when they are ready to receive them. Meet your gifts with love and laughter to fully enjoy them.

JANE'S SOUL MISSION

To reveal truths of life through the written word.
To encourage questioning and seeing from new perspectives.
To create.
To transform.
To spread light.

Guidance for today

Learn to laugh at the foibles and follies of others. The reality of another does not have to impact or become your reality. Stay aware of the truths and untruths within self and all of life. Know thyself to free thyself.

THE CHOICE

Laugh or cry.
See or deny.
Play or fight.
Seek or hide.
Abide or create.
Flee or face.
Rise or descend.

JAYNE MANSFIELD
Actress

Reign in life; be your own sovereign.

This life is a blip on a radar. There is no time to waste. Do today what you have put off for tomorrow. Die empty, that is, empty of all your desires and dreams as they are no longer within you but have found a form of expression in the world. No regrets. No unfinished business. A unique legacy.

Be free of the greatest and silliest limitation in life: a regard for what 'others' think of you. Who are these others? Every time you step out of the box and express any type of uniqueness or authentic expression of you, you will upset someone who does not want your dazzling mirror held up in front of their face. Your light can often be too confronting for others who are intimidated by yours or are confused by it, as they have not yet found a way (within) to claim and radiate their own bright light. Please yourself first, leave the 'others' to please themselves. Be willing to be 'upsetting' enough to challenge any currently accepted limiting paradigms.

JANE'S SOUL MISSION

To embrace the power of being female.
To explore and encourage all expressions of female beauty.
To entertain, uplift and inspire.
To create joy for self and others.
To expand current definitions of what was acceptable and possible.

To love and to care.
To believe in self.

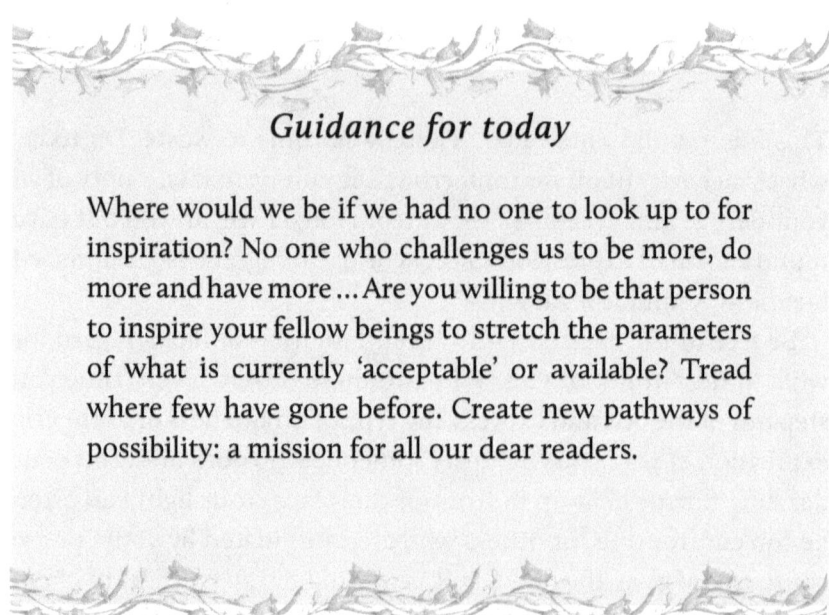

Guidance for today

Where would we be if we had no one to look up to for inspiration? No one who challenges us to be more, do more and have more... Are you willing to be that person to inspire your fellow beings to stretch the parameters of what is currently 'acceptable' or available? Tread where few have gone before. Create new pathways of possibility: a mission for all our dear readers.

THE CHOICE

Live royally and regally. Why not?
Bring some glamour, decadence and hedonism to your days. You are worth it. Let those 'others' know just how valuable you are by the choices you make to support, inspire and uplift you. Perhaps you may even inspire the 'others' to give up settling and instead make grand choices. Grand choices stimulate a grand life. Life on our planet needs awe inducing stimulation!

JESSE OWENS
Olympic Track and Field Athlete

Open to a life worth living ... and celebrating.

Stay in your own lane and then allow your feet to leave the ground. Learn to fly in your own way, my friends. Life wants to give you everything. Seek this 'everything' at every turn. Do not allow your chances to pass you by. Try, fail, rise, reflect, learn and repeat often. You cannot grow where you do not go. Oh, the places you can and should go! Break out of any box that you have allowed yourself to sit in; the view is boring, and you won't get to know what you are truly capable of by sitting there. Life is about discovering all our capabilities and capacities. There are gifts, talents and abilities within you waiting to emerge. Take action to assist your skills into being. Leap out of that box and pack it away today.

JESSE'S SOUL MISSION

To demonstrate possibilities around rising above racial discrimination.
To inspire others to use talents and abilities to create a better life.
To seek freedom and equality.
To discover and express the best of self.

Guidance for today

Sit with yourself in quiet reflection for as long as it takes to start opening to the callings that are within you as part of your life mission. These stirrings are felt and heard on the other side of your fear, your unease and anything else you have allowed to remain in place for numbing you enough to avoid your guidance.

THE CHOICE

Be your own champion in life. Don't wait around for someone else to deliver what you would truly like to see and experience in life. Your desires are yours; you just have to believe in yourself more than you believe in things outside of you.

JOHN F. KENNEDY JR.
*Attorney, Journalist, Magazine Publisher,
Son of the 35th US President*

Life is magnetic, drawing towards you what you most require.

My experience of life was a little complicated and, at the same time, expansive and complex. I had to learn about life from a place of unreality and learn 'reality' from there. My path (my way) was to follow what made me feel alive and content whilst embracing the explorer within me. The love I experienced and shared with others was the catalyst for my growth and wisdom. Our connections should be honoured and treasured. My adventures opened me up to seeing life and its parameters and possibilities. At the end of the day, who and how we love is what our soul remembers and values most deeply and takes beyond this life.

JOHN'S SOUL MISSION

To explore life, self and love from many vantage points.

Guidance for today

Stretch all the elements of your life to stretch yourself. Take risks, expand, open and explore to live fully and to meet all of self. Life is too short to live it from the sidelines. Don't hold back, go forth. Surprisingly, there is nothing of great value to lose.

THE CHOICE

Live largely or hide away in 'safe' obscurity.
Love or miss out on knowing all of you and what you are capable of feeling, being and creating.

JOHN KEATS
English Poet

Believe in and capture the goodness within others and within life.

Romanticism is called for in these modern, somewhat parallel times of both harshness and grace. Allow your heart to soar by believing in the goodness of man and celebrate all occasions of merit to entice more. Goodness and greatness are magnetic and are needed in great quantities today.

Romantics create beautiful childhoods for those in their care and, at the same time, value and connect with their own childhood spirits whenever possible.

Romantics allow their powerful elevated emotions to help connect them with the power of their intuition. Value intuition as much (if not more so) than you do the logical, deductive processes. Creativity and intuition are great bedfellows and bring forth much grace, love and inspiration. These qualities are essential to build positive cultural foundations.

Reconnect with a great friend: nature. Romantics love nature. Nature connects us with peace, awe and beauty—essential ingredients for quality living.

Romantics believe in the impossible and love heroes, particularly those like the phoenix who has risen from the ashes. Become your own hero and believe in superheroes. Society is elevated and thrives when many believe in that which is greater than what is currently presenting in life. Faith and belief in magic and possibility are great antidotes for what currently troubles. Let your imagination soar to transform the mundane into the extraordinary.

Expect the best to receive the best.

Expect magic to receive magic.

Romantics draw beauty into their lives with great ease. Remember that what you focus on increases. Up-level your romanticism for your best living.

JOHN'S SOUL MISSION

To seed love into the culture through the Romanticism movement.

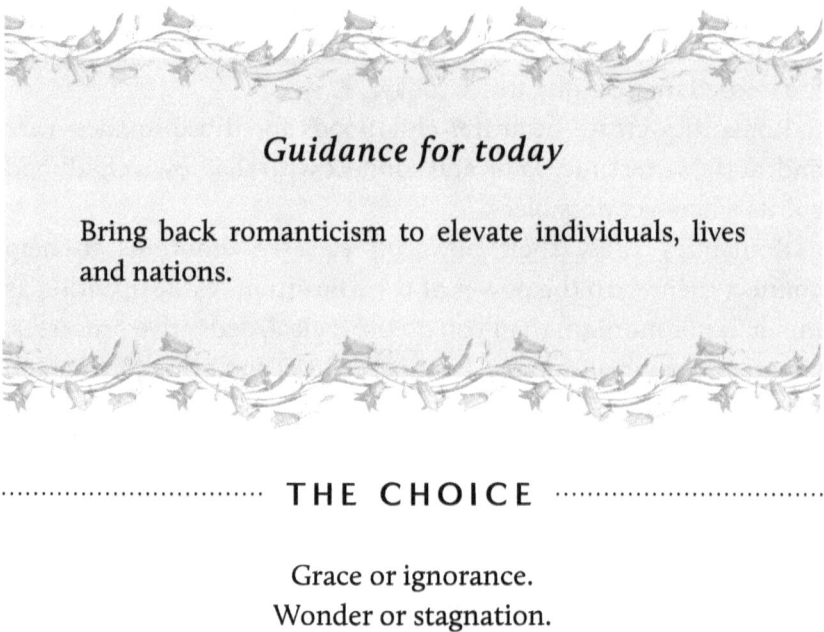

Guidance for today

Bring back romanticism to elevate individuals, lives and nations.

THE CHOICE

Grace or ignorance.
Wonder or stagnation.
Romance or despair.
Love or fear.

JOHN LENNON
Musician, Songwriter, Peace Activist

Peace within for peace in life.

No life is without joy, nor its segues into sadness. The key is to focus more on the light that reveals itself every day, as opposed to the (often) more obvious dark. When we are afraid, we pull back from life. When we are in modes of love, we are open to all that life has to offer.

All opposing states have value. The joy carries us forward in life and the sadness makes us reach harder to connect with the light. The emphasis must pivot radically towards a focus on the love, the light, and the contentment. This encourages peace to become a naturally occurring phenomenon within and then potentially showcasing for the world at large. As a world nation, we will grow and evolve when the collective vibration is raised through more individuals making this choice, this subtle shift.

Keep the picture you have regarding your life always open. Be inquisitive rather than regimented (and therefore limited) in your approach to living. Remember life is what happens to us when we are busy making other plans. That is, the best happens when we cease control and surrender to what is for our highest unveiling good. We do small, the universe does expansive. Align with universal potential instead of ego limitation for your most creative response to soul callings and for activation of your missions and any current supporting requirements.

JOHN'S SOUL MISSION

To create.
To imagine.
To dream a new way into being.
To create awareness of the potential of peace.

Guidance for today

Make it your mission to release (moment to moment) anything that steals your joy. As each person connects with their light, the world around that person changes, impacting the global frequency, such is our combined power.

THE CHOICE

To direct your focus, your energy, towards that which elevates rather than subdues you. Your world and the world at large need the most alive, vital and aware you.

JOHN STEINBECK
Author

Life turns purposefully for those in sync with all occurrences in one's field of experience.

Honour the work you are doing to change self and life. Honour brings grace. Grace is the desired state of being in alignment with great, benevolent cosmic forces. Grace is found most readily within your peace.

Balance tireless toiling with restful rejuvenation. Nature always seeks balance—as must we. All tides flow in and out just as the sun rises and falls. Simple (often powerful) daily occurrences of balance make life work with ease. Every outward expression must have an equal inward expression for the greatest transmission of wisdom. A life lived in balance is a more powerful and enjoyable life. Balance all elements within your soul missions:

Work and play.
Grief and love.
Wounds and healing.
Giving and receiving.
The destruction of old limitations and the creation of the new states of awareness.
Learning from others and opening to inner wisdom.
Retreat and advance.
Inward and outward.
Individual and the whole.
Routine and spontaneity.
Alone time and socialising.
Spend and save.

There is a continuum for every state and experience. Look at where you are currently positioned in any state of living and move in the direction of balance. The foundation for successful soul missions is balance. Life is all about equilibrium as a basis for growth and transformation.

JOHN'S SOUL MISSION

To create worlds for reflection upon through story.
To encourage greater wisdom within many.
To be a voice for truth.
To learn.
To live authentically.
To rise above limitation within self and in life circumstances.
To create balance.
To find attunement through connection with nature.

Guidance for today

Find things you love doing and seek to practise balance within that. Do the same for the tasks you don't enjoy doing. Balance unpopular tasks with pleasurable experiences—some may call it carrot dangling (with self) for greater motivation. You know what works for you to maintain the balance required for successful endeavours.

THE CHOICE

Be a being of balance. Juggling may work for clowns but is rarely sustainable for us.

JOHN WAYNE
Actor

'Courage is being scared to death but saddling up anyway.'
– John Wayne, True Grit (1969)

I loved starring in Western movies as the characters were all very heroic and gung-ho, putting fear on the back burner and trusting that the good guys always win. Light always prevails, my friends. Watch many feel-good movies to remind yourself of this truth if needed. Life is certainly not a Western movie but the freedom to 'be and do' as required to thrive is appealing—minus the necessity for violence. Often, it is not just society that places rules on self as we impose them on ourselves daily through fear of illusionary outcomes. Throw caution to the wind. Free yourself to fire up your authenticity—a great ingredient for connecting with your soul missions. It is a little challenging to meet your soul missions if you are not being the 'you' that helped design them before you were born. Unshackle yourself. There is great fun and power in freedom.

JOHN'S SOUL MISSION

To explore the meaning of life and choice.
To be a voice for freedom of speech.
To question and challenge the status quo to expand thought.
To create through the arts.
To elevate self and others through entertainment.
To bring hope through the screen.
To polarise in order to invoke change.

Guidance for today

Be a modern cowboy or cowgirl: a being who tends and herds others into mutual missions of interest and benefit. There is great strength in collegiality and collaboration.

THE CHOICE

Bend in life and be willing to take the untrodden paths. Remaining stationary and locked into any form of conformity does not create an inspired, expansive life. The world requires your expansiveness and ability to move in new directions, sometimes at a moment's notice. Go where you are called to go. Your missions are beckoning.

JUDITH DURHAM
Singer, Songwriter

We are all seekers of the greatest expression of our light.

Do not be afraid of your soul missions. It is a self-determined universe, and your missions unfold for the highest good of you as a being at the centre. Trust and take comfort in this truth. Stay true to you, to stay on course.

Your work can be conducted quietly and peacefully. Not everyone's version of showing up for their missions involves visibility or public personas. Quiet achievers all around the globe are changing self and enhancing life in their own unique way. Celebrate the quiet, introverted change makers who tirelessly serve without the desire for validation or recognition. Perhaps you are one of these gentle, sensitive souls. Be who you are, dear reader. Allow your missions to unfold from that place within you that feels comfortable as a base. From here, you can stretch and grow as you feel moved to do so. Take your foot off the pedal and allow things to flow through you and towards you in divine timing. Fools rush in where angels fear to tread.

JUDITH'S SOUL MISSION

To create music to uplift and heal.
To connect with love through music.
To seek, be and express love.
To heal towards wholeness.

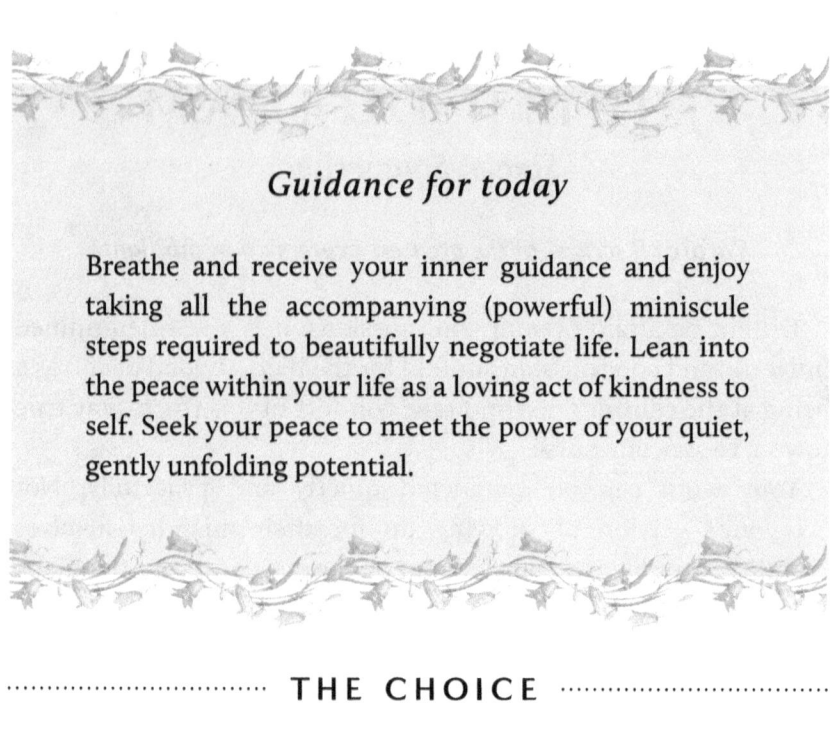

Guidance for today

Breathe and receive your inner guidance and enjoy taking all the accompanying (powerful) miniscule steps required to beautifully negotiate life. Lean into the peace within your life as a loving act of kindness to self. Seek your peace to meet the power of your quiet, gently unfolding potential.

THE CHOICE

Make your peace an integral part of your purpose.

JUDY GARLAND
Actress, Singer

Love ... to be loved.

Be childlike with yourself. You are a precious child of the universe and deserve all the care and love in the world and beyond. If the people and situations in life are not giving you the love and care you need, then you must give it to yourself. The world needs the most loved and cared for version of you because you will then be in a position to do great work. Make it your central mission to find your way back to the love within and allow your callings to flow from there. Your worth in any situation should always be undisputed. Wear your worth proudly and powerfully.

JUDY'S SOUL MISSION

To experience, be and express love.
To create through music and drama.
To explore personal boundaries and power.
To face shadow aspects and heal.
To follow joy, imagination and play to access light.

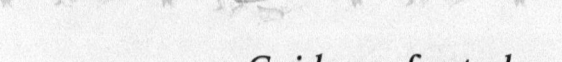

Guidance for today

Find your light in what brings you joy. Use that joy and weave it into your heart space to grow your love. Your love will protect you from the harsh realities of life—it is a force field helping to keep at bay all that you don't require or desire in life. Value and nurture your love above all else.

Be free of false gods promising love. Love must be found within before it can be truly received from sources outside of self. Outer love can be fleeting if not based on the enduring love within.

THE CHOICE

Seek opportunities to reconnect with the most playful, adventurous, light-filled, excited child within. We were love when we arrived on this planet. Make your life's purpose about remembering and sharing this love.

My promise to you is that your love really can heal you back to wholeness. Remove and release all that stands in its way.

JULIAN
Songwriter

Be the love, seek the love, share the love.

We all do things in life that can amount to praise or judgement. Avoid allowing the judgement of others to define you and thus limit you and your ability to take new chances for the advancement of your life. Anyone who judges you is not for you. Find your people—the ones who accept and love all aspects of you. Who we travel through life with greatly influences our contentment and our becoming. Value yourself enough to consciously choose connections to support you and your dreams.

JULIAN'S SOUL MISSION:

To create music for pleasure.
To share gifts to uplift others.
To learn about love within relationships.

Guidance for today

Enjoy your exquisite pearls of success and those received by others. Any good enjoyed by another is transferred in some way into the collective energy field.

Be inspiring and be inspired. Someone's good or success does not exclude you from yours. There is always plenty to go around. In fact, acknowledged success makes success more prevalent all around, such is its potential for transmission. Taking someone off their pedestal of success in any way (thought or deed) chips away at your own potential pedestals of success. Judge or condemn at your own peril. Celebrate others and elevate to new heights.

THE CHOICE

Find your crew, your support network. Love well (with honour and discernment) those who orbit your sphere. You are not for everyone, and everyone is not for you.

JULIE CAMPBELL TATHAM
Author

Weave beautiful stories for self and others through inspired thoughts and deeds.

Find your divine spark. It will be seeded most beautifully by following where your heart leads you. What you love holds the key to your missions. There is no hierarchy in love. If you love what you do, then your work is as important as any work on the planet. Let love lead you each day. Let your love provide a soft place to land, for we all need that in life more than anything else.

JULIE'S SOUL MISSION

To bring mystery and adventure alive for children through literature.
To embrace and create from the inner child.
To create a legacy of love through fantasy.
To mother with care and affection.

Guidance for today

Be single-minded with regards to pursuits (in any area of life) where you are blessed enough to feel inspiration and deep motivation. Inspired living is elevated living.

THE CHOICE

Seek passion and purpose in life to fulfil your days and thus encourage others (by your example) to be open to the possibility of seeking their own joyful inspiration. Inspiration has a resonance that reaches many, even if unseen. You may never know just how much your inspired living influences another. Inspired beings are generally loving, giving, life-enhancing beings. Seek your inspiration. There are many muses within nature, experiences, relationships, literature and within the essence of universal energy. Open your heart to what is truly possible within you and contemporaneously available in your life.

KELLY PRESTON
Actress

*Life is a stage, and we have the roles of actor, director and creator.
This combined creativity knows no bounds.*

I underestimated the power of my beliefs. In this space of hindsight and celestial wisdom, I hold more inspired, expansive beliefs for the evolution of humanity. One of the greatest services you can do for your fellow beings is to hold beliefs that are greater than what is currently evident. We require expansive new beliefs to create expansive new change at a global level. Entertain nothing but great belief in what may be possible to change, even if it is something that has never previously been able to change. Do this on a scale of the largest calibre that you can muster. If you have a large platform, use it well. Inspire all those you encounter to believe that no 'thing' is impossible in all ways and in all fields. Believe in radical new possibilities for health, technology, peace and all that has the potential to enhance life on Earth.

KELLY'S SOUL MISSION

To live and connect from the heart.
To be an exemplar of leading through love.
To parent self and others.
To learn about and apply the transformative power of
the beauty of love to uplift life.
To laugh and play.

Guidance for today

Wear life lightly, placing significance only on expressions of love. There is power in each moment of earthly living. Too much power is lost in pointless thinking and worry. Nothing can change from this undesirable state. Instead, believe (even in the face of insurmountable odds and no evidence thereof) that what you desire is possible. Believe in the best for self and others in all moments. Holding the space for another, despite their lack of belief in self or apparent futility, is one of our most powerful, life-changing and miracle-inducing superpowers we can own and activate.

THE CHOICE

Identify, release and up-level your 'non beliefs' to live your best life for self and others.

*Author's note:
Those we worry about do not require our worry. They require our faith. Convert your worry to wisdom and share that instead.

LAURA INGALLS WILDER
Author

*Find home within your heart and create a
beautiful hearth from there.*

Simplicity is the message I wish to impart here today. Reconnect with the quiet, the ease, the slowness and the simple joys in life. The pace of modern life is so fast that it can interfere with hearing the musings of the soul. Beings who are quiet and peaceful connect with their soul missions with greater ease and less fuss. Grandiose is not always best as it is too easy for this state to be interwoven with ego dominance. Much has improved and advanced in society, but we can also look to the past to remember simple pleasures and tasks that connect us to presence and creativity—two of the most powerful and healing states.

Preparing a meal for loved ones, seeing buds bloom in your own garden, watching the night sky for a shooting star, creating something with your hands or writing a letter are all examples of tasks that are gentle and calming and much needed in modern times.

LAURA'S SOUL MISSION

To share stories to teach, heal and entertain.
To live from love and truth.
To be free to express soul gifts and desires.
To find a voice and use it to serve all of life.

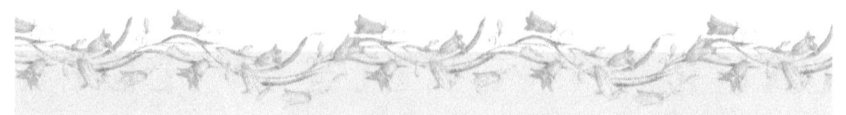

Guidance for today

Slow down, sister and brother. Do less and be more. Many of you spread yourselves too thin and circumvent your effectiveness. Live life with purpose and intent; with calm, quieting undercurrents flowing through all occurrences whenever and wherever possible. Earth and her inhabitants will benefit from your peace—as will you.

THE CHOICE

Let peace be your guide.
What would your peace have you do on this day?
Where would peace take you on this day?
What would your peace have you express on this day?

LAUREN BACALL
Actress

Flow with the waters of your life as you are the one setting the course on which to sail.

Do not resist life as it is steering you in the direction of your greatest capacity for activating your soul missions and for living them through love, joy and abundance of all kinds. Just listen and learn (even half as much more than you do currently) and you could forego the need to 're-learn and re-route' through discomfort and suffering. The suffering occurs when you don't listen to the voice of your soul and resist releasing and unlearning everything in the way of your true becoming. Make the demand to become and express all that you came here to be and create.

Be fun and flirtatious with a sparkle in your eye and love in your heart. Play, lighten up. The collective energies are very intense right now as the dark is being revealed and forced to the surface for release. The lighter you can be, the more power is infused into the collective energy to shift what needs to be shifted for greater awakening, love and conscious possibility for life on earth.

Life is a party and we are all invited. The only stipulation for attending is that you do not wear a mask of any kind. Authentic individuality is the dress code and freedom is the theme. With these attributes in place, a fun time is guaranteed, although there will be many challenges and initiations along the way. These 'tests' will serve the purpose of making the celebrations even more appealing, strength-inducing and gratitude-heightening. What a party! This party is full of VIP guests and there will be much collaboration and sharing of personal stories of awakening, triumph and successfully explored missions. Enjoy this party for what it is, for what is presented. Don't wish it to be any other way. It is just as it needs to be on this day, on this night, at this time. Live life in this moment, allowing the rest to take care of itself. You have the most talented behind-the-scenes party planners imaginable. Embrace the power of the unseen, unknown elements within your life.

Know who you are and wear all of it proudly.

LAUREN'S SOUL MISSION

To learn about and express personal power.
To create and manifest dreams and desires.
To inspire through the arts.
To live in abundance in order to open others to possibility.
To love.
To radiate light and potential.
To question and challenge current viewpoints within self and society.
To create.
To lead by example.
To portray strong female dynamics to inspire change.
To be authentic.
To demonstrate freedom of voice and choice.

Guidance for today

Live in a state of readiness to receive your dreams. Act powerfully and confidently until you catch up with the inherent strength within your soul.

The acknowledgment of your power will send signals to your soul that you are ready to receive and activate your personal soul missions. Your dreams are little callings from your soul, always indicative of your missions throughout various stages of your life. As you change and up-level, your dreams and missions will transform to new levels as well. You expand, life expands, as does your potential and the impact you make on and for life.

THE CHOICE

Water the garden within through whatever nourishment you require. You need your blooms to flourish at peak periods in life when your missions call most strongly. Embrace all the seasons within your living. What appears as dormancy is often great regeneration and future blooming in the making. Choose to be a VIP in your life, for you are. You never were and never will be anything but first-class. Know that, in all your days, no matter where you are, or what your perceived current 'position' is in life, that you deserve the best. Please know that life is conspiring to give you more than you desire. To fully receive what is yours, gently step away from anything you have in place to limit you. Give yourself permission to free yourself from those who attempt to block your path. Choose all of you, for you. Be it all, to receive it all.

LEO TOLSTOY
Author

Find the truth just below the surface of things to avoid missing what is yours to know.

I always found much learning in my response to different viewpoints and values within cultures other than my own. Here I found many concealed gems that I could absorb. I could take new truths from experience and add this to my own sphere of knowledge to enhance my wisdom. I came to know that a great truth for me was knowing that I didn't know and therefore I was always open to fresh input, especially when it challenged any current set of beliefs that I was holding onto about self, others and life occurrences in general. There is so much illusion woven into our world, so I avoided latching onto any prevailing truth for too long. Allow your truth to evolve and change as a companion to all your experiences in all your days. There is no growth in drawing conclusions (no matter how popular it may be) or in absolute, immovable knowing. Grant yourself the freedom to open up to ideas that come from out of left field, considering what they may have to offer. Value fresh input. Just as a child is open to new discoveries and ideas that are far-fetched and imagination-stretching, you can be, too. Remember that what were once crazy ponderings (over many decades ago) sowed seeds for the brilliance of today. Be intrigued rather than threatened by the novel and unfamiliar. At the same time, do not be the effect of the truth of others. If it sparks greater awareness within you, that's great. If not, let it go. Let it be.

LEO'S SOUL MISSION

To seek truth.
To learn about self and life and infuse this wisdom within literature for the highest good.
To understand and enhance human nature.
To create.

Guidance for today

Love not what you know but what you are yet to learn. Be a seeker of all the wisdom that is available to you in this lifetime and share it in some way. Infinitesimally small or on a large scale—however you are called to express truth throughout your mission is just perfect. Open your voice by finding the freedom from fear within and share it. Create your life from a deep foundation of personal, ever-evolving truth.

THE CHOICE

Truth is a gift for self and the world. Will you bravely look more deeply to find what is real and true for you?
Use truth of all kinds to enhance life.
Whatever the current mass consensus is, take a twist and turn in a new direction to find hidden truth treasures.

LEONARDO DA VINCI
Inventor, Mathematician, Artist, Scientist, Engineer, Architect, Theorist, Polymath

Be a student of all things and a master of many.

Human capacity is unlimited. Imagination is unlimited. Anything that can be imagined can be created if it is for the highest good.

There is an intelligence in life that runs through all things and a corresponding potential for brilliance within the hearts and minds of all beings. Be a seeker of knowledge. Knowledge repeatedly combined with awareness creates the most transformative kinds of wisdom that often miraculously converts to genius.

LEONARDO'S SOUL MISSION

To bring things and ideas of the future into current times to spark curiosity, awareness and innovation.
To leave behind a legacy of beauty, thought, creativity, magic, mystery and possibility.
To transform life into a greater expression.
To encourage questioning of the current reality to open up to a new reality.
To imagine, to create.
To receive divine downloads to enhance the human condition.

Guidance for today

Learn something new every day of your life. Be something new. Reinvent self and life at every opportunity. Stagnation and atrophy cannot limit life if learning, seeking, curiosity, creativity and wonder are central to one's existence. Come alive to the exquisite potential that exists within you and all of life.

What legacy will the activation of your soul mission leave behind on planet Earth?

THE CHOICE

Be magnetic to miracles. Be what you seek to attract or create. Rise up to meet your superpowers, draw them down from the stars, from the heavens, from the cosmos, from the furthest galaxy—from wherever you can reach. Be one with universal creation and therefore unlimited.

LINDA
Actress

*Seek your inner radiance and, from there, find its
outward expression to uplift self and others.*

Dial down life to meet the power of simplicity. Aggrandisement is not always best. The simplest acts and deeds often have the most impact. Often, this is because small acts occur in the moment with a spontaneity that arises from the heart. Kind words have the power to transform. Compliments are gifts for the soul. Opening a door for another makes them feel valued. A thank-you card makes the recipient feel seen and appreciated. There are a plethora of ways that we can enact our soul missions just by being us, daily. Each time we indulge in random acts of service (that call to us via our powerful internal guidance system), we create beautiful life-enhancing swirls that resonate with love.

LINDA'S SOUL MISSION

To uplift others.
To create and express beauty.
To entertain.
To love.
To heal.
To learn from the contrasts of life.

Guidance for today

Invoke the power of your smile. It is an instant energy uplifter for self and others. Your smile has the power to light up the person whom you bestow this gift upon. That person then feels good and is more inclined to make others feel good. Pay lots of smiles and great vibes forward.

THE CHOICE

Life is sweet, make it even more so with the sweetest of acts.

LINDA MCCARTNEY
Musician, Activist, Author, Photographer

Capture all of life within your heart, for your mind alone will not infuse your life with the full power of your love.

Be many things in life. There are too many opportunities and too many experiences available to make a subconscious choice to limit life in any way. Avoid deciding, 'I am this / I do that'. Allow your choices to change and evolve right alongside your own evolution in consciousness. Know in your heart that you are worthy of experiencing all you desire and that you are capable of many amazing things, many of which will not even be on your current radar. As you open up to life, life will provide you with new doorways to walk through. Walk a beautiful path with creativity, love and abundance infused within all your missions.

LINDA'S SOUL MISSION

To create through artistic expression.
To be an advocate for animal rights.
To love and nurture.
To find and express personal voice.
To move from ego to heart-based functioning.
To be and express the freedom of authenticity and choice.

Guidance for today

Tune into your heart. Breathe into it. Momentarily cease all thinking. Just feel. Fill your heart space with love-light. Imagine all that love-light brightening as you simultaneously connect with loving thoughts, feelings and images. Build this power of you, then perceive this energy radiating deeply within to all those untouched places and then spreading outwards as far as you can send it. Be heart-based today and in all your days to activate the soul knowledge and gifts for supporting your daily missions which in turn support your life missions.

THE CHOICE

Mind dominance or heart power. The first comes naturally, the second requires great vigilance and even greater reward.

LISA MARIE PRESLEY
Singer, Songwriter

Large lives can be lived quietly and truthfully.

No matter who you are or what your current life circumstances are, don't ever be the shadow side of the moon to someone else's supernova. If this is where you choose to orbit, it is very difficult to let your own star burn brightly. There is a greatness within, unique to every being. We all come from the same source and have our own unique note to play. Avoid attempting to emulate those you admire (or are influenced by) as it becomes a distraction from your own authentic evolution. Discover your own power to create.

LISA'S SOUL MISSION

> To navigate truth amongst untruths.
> To love.
> To create authentically.
> To promote healing and love through music.
> To find joy in creative expression.
> To understand the polarity of life.
> To open up to the light via the catalyst of suffering.

Guidance for today

I could not breathe without comparison and it weighed heavily. It meant each time I dipped my toe in fresh water, it was soaked in fear.

Comparison keeps us limited as it fuels self-doubt which is the greatest handbrake in life. Give yourself the gift of freedom from comparison and you will know true peace and meet the power and joy of your own authenticity. The world needs millions of possibilities. Be willing to be 'one in a million'—whatever that looks like for you. Your soul knows the way. Quiet the white noise to receive the whispers of insight connecting you to your life goals and mission. Your mission (not anyone else's) is exactly what you need and desire— even if you do not know this yet. You will ... as you allow the words within this book to open you up to yourself and your remembering.

THE CHOICE

Create your own unique legacy. Be inspired to be great by the work of others. However, do this without feeling the need to become a version of any other being, for it will lead to a paler expression of you than what is truly possible.

LOUISA MAY ALCOTT
Author

Tend your pastures well, treating the earth you walk on with respect.

Karma occurs not just within relationships but also in response to the treatment of Mother Earth. The land and seas are for the enjoyment and nourishment of all. All undertakings connected to the Earth should be carried out for the highest good of all—and for the planet as a whole entity. Every Earth action has a corresponding Earth consequence. Take care of your own plot and be aware of what is occurring on the four corners of the globe, for it is also your home and the home of the generations that will follow in your line. Health is impacted in many places by the toxic nature of soils, cultivation and husbandry practises. A great review is most necessary. Become aware of what is occurring and have a voice where possible. Avoid buying those products that do not add to the health of Earth's inhabitants. It will not be until unhealthy food products stop selling as there is no longer any demand for them that changes are made. Money and profits speak very loudly.

LOUISA'S SOUL MISSION

To challenge current gender and societal norms.
To encourage greater awareness amongst fellow souls in exploring the meaning of life.
To entertain and inspire through writing.
To demonstrate the power of creativity.
To draw attention to injustice and malpractice.

Guidance for today

Food sources are somewhat contaminated in many locations throughout the world. As much as possible, create your own plot for growing the essentials. The closer you can eat from a trusted source, the better. Create awareness and demand where possible that your food is clean and free from interference. Healthy bodies contribute to the creation of rich, fruitful lives. It is a human right that food be grown and cultivated with integrity and transparency.

·············· **THE CHOICE** ··············

Choose health. Every choice counts. The human
body is phenomenal. Support it as best you can for a
pleasurable and productive life. Your missions need
your wellness and vitality.

··

LOUISE HAY
Founder of Hay House Publishing, Spiritual Teacher and Author

Heal you, heal your life, change the world.

Wellness is key. A sick population is an easily controlled population and does not as readily come into soul alignment or establish the highest connection with cosmic power. Our world needs our full potential. Most importantly, you need your full potential to create the life you are here for: the life of your dreams, in fact, a life beyond your wildest dreams. The universe is unlimited and we are an integral part of this intelligent, complex, vast, infinitely creative system. Face your fears, look within your anxieties for your wisdom. Forgive. Heal your past and your wounds. There is no time to waste on nonsense as you have much to achieve. Heal yourself to connect with the energy and vitality that is most desirous for your best journey towards meeting your soul missions.

As the sun rises, make each day count—and always count your blessings to manifest more and feel even more deeply into your wellness.

Life is really very simple. You attract what you are. What you desire is also seeking you; you just need to align your thoughts, feelings, emotions and actions with what you seek. Your vibration, your inner essence, is everything. It is the guidance signal, the beacon drawing the life meant for you, to you. Allow inspiration (spirit moving through you and for you) to pave the way throughout your beautiful life.

LOUISE'S SOUL MISSION

To heal self and lead the way for the world to do the same.

To identify and share the root cause of unease.

To understand the metaphysical nature of illness.

To promote an understanding of the mind, heart and body connection.

To write to heal, to teach, to transform.

To create platforms to support the power of the word to inspire and transform.

To lead by example.

To enhance the vibration of the world.

Guidance for today

Never underestimate the power of your thoughts. We create our lives one increment at a time via our thoughts and their corresponding emotions. This combination creates our energy field—a complex vibrational system. It is advantageous for our soul missions to maintain a high vibration for drawing in our highest good. Thoughts have a powerful frequency and radiate out into the universe, sometimes as gentle ripples and other times as shockwaves. Take charge of your thinking to take charge of your life.

THE CHOICE

Create the world you desire via the thoughts you think, the energy you receive and radiate, and the alignment you establish with your soul and its higher calling.

MAE WEST
Actress

Unique is divine.

Crack the code to the abundance (of all that is great in life) that awaits you on the other side of the 'you' that you were taught to be. Who are you really? What are you here to create, be, instigate and change? How have you defined and created yourself? Do you have a commitment to being good? Are you the people pleaser or the caretaker? Does your life revolve around seeking approval or validation? Are you willing to be the spark of uniqueness you truly are? Identifying patterns that potentially run us is the first step to freedom. We are all potential transformers.

Learn to see the forest through the trees. Live life with a bird's-eye view. Expand out, go infinite into the unknown realms of possibility. Marvel in the mysterious. You are free in the unknown; your heart is unconstricted, and your mind is capable of connecting with cosmic wisdom. Be of the Earth but connected to the stars. Draw heaven closer to Earth with your great reach. Be the giant Earth being that you truly are. We need a world of 'giants'—those that are free of small-mindedness and externally imposed limitations. Take your true place in this world. Mankind and womankind await your presence at the grand table of life. What are you here to savour? Dine on all that is presented for you with wisdom, discernment, enjoyment and gratitude.

MAE'S SOUL MISSION

To explore and expand the limitations in place for female expression.
To free the divine feminine by incorporating the divine masculine.
To heal in order to invoke wholeness.

Guidance for today

Push the boundaries a little to create new ones with more unique and expandable edges. Say 'yes' to every 'no' that has been subliminally or intentionally placed upon you. No being can say 'no' to what your soul came here to achieve—only you have that authority.

THE CHOICE

Emerge from the darkness that was never yours to begin with. Light up, little stars! Brighten the world.

MARCO POLO
Explorer, Writer

Fall in love with the unknown as it is where possibility is born.

Ignite the fire within your soul through exploration of all kinds. Explore not only new territories and vistas but explore your gifts, talents, abilities and the great wisdom deep within your soul. Explore the limits of your courage and then stretch some more. Explore your beliefs to see where there is room for more expansion. Explore your triggers and wounds to come to know that they need not define or limit you, especially if you decide to forgive, heal and release them. Create your own map and follow it to design an adventurous life for meeting many of your great missions. Life is the adventure you make it.

MARCO'S SOUL MISSION

To explore what the world has to offer and interpret and share these findings.
To contribute to the knowledge of the geography, resources and people of the world.
To embrace courage.
To venture into the unknown.

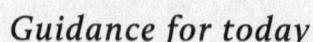

Guidance for today

Begin each day with a spark in your heart. Ask, 'What adventure will best serve my missions this day for the highest good?' Enjoy what unfolds. Love the mystery and surprise within the unknown dimensions of living. Surrender is such a treat and so much more fun than controlled limitation.

Set sail where few have gone before. Embrace your inner trailblazer in any field of endeavour.

THE CHOICE

Get to know your inner gypsy. Where would they like to go? What would they like to do? Life is too short to remain in one place, doing the same thing. There is much to see, much to experience and many individuals to meet. Be an adventurous explorer of life. Bodies like movement and souls love it even more. Creative beings love the inner fire ignited through adventure.

MARCUS AURELIUS
Roman Emperor, Philosopher

*'You have power over your mind—not outside events.
Realise this, and you will find strength.'*
– Marcus Aurelius

Find your strength. This life requires an acceleration of your power. Life is overwhelming if we retreat into our weaknesses: doubt, fear and lack of worth and love. Quiet the noise. Don't listen to the world outside of you until you know and trust yourself. Trust yourself by making the daily commitment to push back negativity into the light. Fill your mind with great thoughts about you, your life and others. Create a euphoric mind to create a loving heart and blissful life.

MARCUS'S SOUL MISSION

To create new thought.
To understand the workings and power of the mind.
To lead self and others to greatness within and in one's living and response to life.
To teach, leaving a legacy of writings to enhance evolution.

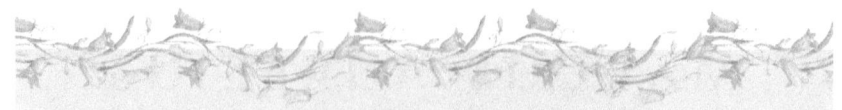

Guidance for today

Be aware in all your days. Know that everything we hear is an opinion, not a fact. Everything we see is perspective, not truth. Stay open to all new information to enhance the possibility of developing your own treasure trove of liberating, loving and powerful wisdom. This wisdom will guide you forward, enabling you to live through successful missions, thus creating a full, abundant life.

THE CHOICE

Monitor your mind because it controls the emotions that can rule a life and own a body.

MARIE ANTOINETTE
Queen of France

Lead life on your terms, allowing it to be a true expression of you.

As a child, I was thrown into an adult life, somewhat ill-prepared, but with an open heart. Let the child within you enjoy childhood and protect the childhoods of those in your sphere. Childhood should be magical, providing the foundation for a powerfully effective life. Childhood is essential for cultivating the imagination and the creativity that is a crucial component of purposeful living and its associated connection to soul missions. Creativity places us in the right space to receive our deep wisdom, our deep knowing and the blueprint for our soul missions. Aspire to keep your childhood and 'fantastical mind' alive in all your adult days. Being imaginative and inspired opens you to your true potential and has a miraculous way of drawing what you require for a soul-led life to your doorstep. Play along with life, regardless of what is presented.

MARIE'S SOUL MISSION

To know self and to live as a true soul expression.
To expose others to a greater variety of life options and potential.
To stimulate new thought and awakening.
To draw attention to the limitations of the times.
To keep childhood alive within adult living.

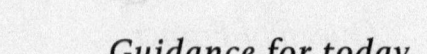

Guidance for today

Do not leave this planet feeling like your life was only half-lived, or worse, defined by or managed by the opinions and expectations of others.

Be true to yourself so life has a greater chance of being true to you. Life is a mismatch for those who don't connect with and truthfully express their own individuality and authenticity.

THE CHOICE

Live life free from the influence or opinion of others. They do not know what you came here for … only you do. Your mission may elude you if you are choosing to live someone else's life or from someone else's shoes. You do not benefit from such distraction.

MARILYN MONROE
Actress

Women are creators of beauty. Free them in all corners of the globe. Let them create.

My story is for me to tell, and it is time.

My childhood was less than ideal but no different to that of many children who had parents who could not parent themselves.

I was a product of a fractured world in moving form.

My light was strong but with each passing decade, my light was used to serve others, to my own detriment.

My movies were to bring joy, to bring love, to remember innocence, lightness, free-spiritedness and kindness.

My life served to remind women of the consequences of not acknowledging and using their own power. It was never a man's world (despite appearances). Women are, and always will be, the greatest conduits for love and close to all that is sacred.

MARILYN'S SOUL MISSION

To expose the patriarchy, revealing where female power was being sublimated.

To stir the winds of change.

To wake up women to their own places of subservience.

To encourage the reclamation of female power: the power of their beauty, sensuality and gifts.

To embrace the divine feminine.

To showcase the dark, life force-depleting and destructive power of drugs.

Guidance for today

See where you can be of service to womankind. Act. We are all one. None of us are truly free until all of us are free. Collaborate, rather than compete. Community is an avenue for our most useful shared transformative powers.

THE CHOICE

Be an advocate for women.
Find those places where female power has been taken hostage. Be a vehicle for change, creating freedom for women who are still 'locked up' by the constraints of living within an archaic, male-dominated culture.

MARTIN LUTHER KING JR.
Activist

Egalitarianism is the way of the light.

Dear people,
Thank you for being here today and allowing your soul to be stirred towards the actions your missions most require. Each of your missions contains magic threads that are interwoven with the missions of many others. Take note of coincidences, synchronicity and the people that come into your life, for they are all signposts guiding you to where you need to be, doing what you most need to be doing. Flow into your soul callings and accompanying missions. Do not fear what you are here to do. Instead, love it all into being. You were born for great things and grand adventures. Honourable, heart-based choices will gift you a life beyond your largest dreams. Move the shadows out of the way and feel into the ease of your light. Life is far easier, way simpler and more supportive of you than you can currently imagine. I pray you find your ease, flow and magic momentum.

MARTIN'S SOUL MISSION

To promote freedom and equality.
To use one's voice to alchemise dark into light.
To create awareness around human rights.

Guidance for today

Know that what occurs for any group of people occurs for all groups of people, such is the interconnectedness of all beings.
Seek your truth and you are helping others to seek their truth.
Free yourself from that which binds and assist others to break free of their binds.
Base your life on love and others will be moved by your loving presence.
Follow what's bringing you joy and help yourself and others to find their joy—bringing forth circumstances to support your soul missions with greater rapidity.
Joy is a soul mission catalyst.

THE CHOICE

Be heard. Use your voice to create a better world.
Words spoken for the highest good have the support
of the hidden realms. We hear you; we back you.

MARY QUANT
Fashion Designer

Fashion a designer life for yourself.

Light up and light up some more. Your greatest mission in this lifetime is to find what you love and draw in abundance of all kinds whilst doing it. Your work should inspire you and motivate you to serve in some way. Contribution is woven into your missions; service occurs naturally when you find what you love and connect deeply with your purpose. We came here to change life on Earth. Thank you for accepting your missions, as they are not easy to navigate during these tumultuous times of transition. Keep striving to be the best version of you, knowing that designing and creating your best life is part of this. Breathe often and take lots of breaks. Great service requires great restoration. Make your self-care an integral part of your life. Output of any kind needs inner rejuvenation in ways unique to you. It's okay if some days it all feels too much, and you'd like some time offshore or even off Earth. You are supported, guided and loved more than you know. Your efforts contain great reward in this world and beyond this world. Keep showing up for what life requires of you, dear creative, most talented designer.

MARY'S SOUL MISSION

To promote creativity.
To design clothes to encourage dressing as a loving expression of self.
To encourage celebration of female beauty and form through creative style.
To challenge accepted societal norms to establish

greater freedom and authentic living.
To light up self and others.
To lead by example.
To love self, life and others.

Guidance for today

Be an active and creative participant in your life. Avoid living your life for others or having it governed by any other being. Many of you work for others. Still be you. Keep part of you separate from your employment and when you leave each day, tune into yourself and where your dreams are going to take you next. Avoid allowing your work to consume you unless it is a passionate love. Even then, always create space for intrigue, newness and change. Allow new beginnings to be a regular part of your existence.

THE CHOICE

Design greatness into your days. Start by acknowledging it within self. Ask, 'What is great about me today, acknowledged and unacknowledged?' Keep opening to more of the mystery and magic of you, for it holds the keys to your untapped potential.

MARY
Queen of Scots

There is great fanfare as each soul awakens to the truth of themselves and their purpose on Earth. Purpose-filled lives change the world.

Do not get caught up in the random events of life. It can be quite hazardous and tumultuous when placing too much significance on Earthly matters or focusing too much energy on Earthly personas. Look heavenward for your wisdom, clarity and power. Draw these qualities within to activate your true self. This true self is the one that can cruise through life with relative ease with the assistance of synchronicity powerfully connecting the dots, moving us to where we need to be and doing what is in our best interests for our soul missions. We need to live 'above' our lives, running them from our higher selves if we wish to rise above the rabble, insanity and confusion. Life can be a hot and cold mess if not lived through divine connection and guidance. Living through the higher self is in stark contrast to being in the grips of the ego. The ego does not understand our higher self. In its desperate attempts to keep us safe from the greatness of us (where we take beautiful, calculated risks bringing change), it keeps us running around in circles in a perpetual state of unease and uncertainty. In this space, we struggle within ourselves to connect with our purpose in life and trust in its unfolding. We go down rabbit holes that we then need to clamber out of whilst maintaining an unfavourable sense of disorientation. Move away from ego noise, be still, be you. Awaken, for there is an easier way. Return to the truth of you and how life really works to serve you best, activating your soul path and missions. Our higher selves position us in life with skill and unimaginable expertise— with a great degree of magic intertwined in the process. Connection with your soul mission does not have to be hard. It is as natural as being born. Intend on claiming your soul wisdom today and the universe will support you every step of the way.

MARY'S SOUL MISSION

To find order when there was none.
To direct my life when others were intent on directing it for me.
To meet the power of my inner child and connect this with my adult power.
To connect with something greater to make the impossible possible.
To lead from darkness to the light.
To explore the complexities of human nature.

Guidance for today

Lead from the heart that is connected to the higher self and infused with love—the most simple and powerful formula for successfully living with purpose, ease and joy.

THE CHOICE

Make the demand for yourself that you spend more and more time each day functioning from your higher self as opposed to your ego. Use unease and love as your guiding scale; love being the indicator that you are in your higher super self, and unease being an alarm bell indicating that it's time to stop, reflect and redirect your thinking and attitude away from potential ego traps. You want to live in paradise (as your power is greatest here) even if you haven't acknowledged it yet. Your higher self knows the way. Step away from the small self and don't sweat the small stuff. Bigger picture, dear reader, bigger picture.

MATA HARI
Exotic Dancer

*Keep evolving. Be undefinable and unstoppable and
all your missions will bloom.*

Who am I today and what would I like to create for fun and love? Start each day with questions (such as this powerful one) to expand your life rather than shut aspects of it down. Lean into your magnificence instead of your smallness (your fear) as often as you are willing. Magnificence moves mountains and often creates your own equivalent creations of magnitude.

For further growth, reflect on your family lineage every now and then. You will learn a great deal about yourself, opening to much awareness and concurrent liberation. Honestly review how, why and in what circumstances you may be repeating familial patterns ... or are you transforming them into new expressions and potential? If you are reading this book, you are no doubt a great transformer of inherited (by osmosis) limitations. Celebrate this! What are you now choosing to be and do that no one in your family has been willing or able to be and create? We applaud you, for you are helping to create a new legacy for those around you and for those that follow. Each small tweak or release in family conditioning opens you up to new, previously unseen realms of possibility. As you evolve, humanity evolves, such is the power of collective connection.

MATA'S SOUL MISSION

To express beauty and sensuality.
To love.

To create.
To transform self.
To dance.
To bring joy through entertainment.
To seek pleasure and contentment.
To take risks to grow and evolve.
To be an authentic expression of self.
To be free.
To inspire people to open up to more.
To encourage female empowerment and liberation.

Guidance for today

Make finding what you love to do and be central to your existence. Everything else important in your life will follow from this foundation of love.

THE CHOICE

Be free to be all that you came here to be. Reach for the full spectrum of the potential within you ... with no excuses and no regrets. What will you do tomorrow that you didn't do today?
Hold yourself accountable. Listen to your inner guidance and, most importantly, act upon it. Guidance without action is void of its inherent potential.

MAY GIBBS
Children's Author, Cartoonist, Illustrator

Be the creative spark your life desires.

Explore your own version of creativity to enliven your days. The way our creativity is opened is as unique as our actual creations. Often, we require multiple forms of inspiration. Find what combination of conditions stirs your creativity. You may need exercise and time in nature. You may need music and inspirational literature. You may need a change of scenery and great company. You may need deep rest followed by dancing. Find your way to your creativity and enjoy how inspiration seems to just drop in. Each day we choose to create anew (whether it be in the form of a hairstyle, outfit, poem, recipe, home space, art or any one of the many creative choices available to us), we are truly living.

Love and dream all manner of creations into existence. Use the power of your imagination to visualise new creations. There is no endpoint to our creative potential. In fact, you will find that embracing one form of creativity gives birth to many more expressions and styles:

An actress may venture into singing.
A sportsperson may write a memoir.
An artist may design buildings.
An author may produce a movie.
A gardener may become a florist.
A chef may design kitchenware.
A fashion designer may create a jewellery line.
A model may become a stylist.

Creations provide the fertile soil for much more to bloom. Be prepared to be surprised and even in awe of what you produce in life, and for life, once you've made the commitment to open your creativity. Paint your life canvas with much to admire and cherish. Everything you create has an energy. Allow your creativity to bless yourself and those around you with a timeless legacy.

Nurture your creative spirit as you would anything you value in life.

MAY'S SOUL MISSION

To bring joy and peace to the world through beautiful stories and images.
To embrace creativity.
To love vision into reality.

Guidance for today

Absorb the amazing creative works of those you admire to stimulate your own propensity towards creation. We never need to be or create just one thing when so much is available and possible. Stretch to grow.

THE CHOICE

Create through optimism, confidence and joy.
Your creations need your faith, not your doubt
in their value.

MAYA ANGELOU
Spiritual Teacher, Author

*'Do the best you can until you know better.
Then when you know better, do better.'
– Maya Angelou*

Meet self and others where you (and they) are currently at without judgement. We are all on different stages of the journey; support yourself through self-care and any form of education that leads to more awareness, wisdom and contentment. Don't underestimate the power of feeling good as it is a powerful foundation for being and attracting great living and, at the same time, having a positive impact on those who surround you. It is far easier to wield your light and recognise your gifts, talents and abilities when feeling good. Utilise your earned evolving wisdom to help others awaken to their love and power through the service you provide in your world. Your service provides enduring light to self and others. Honour all the contributions that you make to enhance and move life forward.

MAYA'S SOUL MISSION

To open self and others to their spiritual essence.
To leave behind a better world than the one born into.
To be a voice for freedom of all kinds.
To create works that teach, heal, inspire, elevate and transform.

Guidance for today

Be kind to yourself. Be more committed to seeing and acknowledging what is right and beautiful about you than you are on attempting to locate and dissect any perceived flaws. If you focus enough on the greatness of you, rather than on the 'other', you will find things often miraculously dissipate or transmute into something else entirely.

THE CHOICE

Be a force of light for this world. Gather other light workers and shine light on the shadowy aspects witnessed in life. All in life contains the potential for transformation. First, we need to be brave enough to take a look at what we have previously had no desire to see. Witness and wield my friends. Use your increasing power well.

MICHAEL BOND
Author

Make peace with you, just for you.

That fragile little piece within you that is easily hurt, scared or wounded, care for this aspect of you as you would a young, innocent child.

How does he or she need to be nurtured back to love and a greater, more truthful connection with self?

What lie about self, did he or she buy that isn't real?

Where is he or she being unnecessarily disparaging or unkind to self?

What does the hurt child within you require most to thrive today?

Become your own wise counsel. All that you need to heal to become your best self for your soul missions is within you. Heed the little cries of pain within, that if you tend to them rather than deny them, will set you free to be more than you imagined possible. Journey back to heightened wellbeing to be most effective in life. Do a daily inventory of how you are feeling. Make choices about where you will go, what you will do and who you will see that reflect your inner needs. Taking care of your inner world creates the potential for greatness within life.

MICHAEL'S SOUL MISSION

To elevate self and others.
To bring joy through writing.
To create warmth.
To bring the healing power of fictional story to others.

To invoke lightness of being.
To promote a love of literature and reading.

Guidance for today

Make a decision and then immediately honour the wisdom you had in the moment to make the choice. Second guessing ourselves seeds doubt, worry and shame. It is easier to navigate our soul missions with love and trust in self as the primary creative underpinning force.

Many make a choice (that they are initially content with) and then torture themselves after the fact. This is not necessary, my friend. Own your intuition and back your choices. You can always choose again. Choose prolifically. Choice is the foundation of creation.

THE CHOICE

Perceive life and all its associated challenges with
lightness of being. You are here to be happy.
Your personal, divine right for contentment is
woven within all soul missions. Happiness and peace
are the endgames, even if duress often needs to be
overcome before one meets the full spectrum of
fulfilment and joy.

MICHAEL HUTCHENCE
Musician

Too much excess within INXS.

My life was a paradox: so much pain, so much love. My talent became my master rather than my servant. The excess of all things that were not in my best interests became my downfall. My advice is to cherish simplicity, to seek peace along with purpose. Keep your desires aligned with the essence of who you are evolving into becoming. From here, trust life to support you as you will never fully know where you are heading and how you are transforming. I needed to spend more time in a preparatory cocoon. I wasn't quite ready to meet the full power and influence of my gifts. Check in with yourself hourly if necessary. Avoid going down paths that take you away from who you are, for it is too easy to become lost in this cavernous space. Higher self-activation versus ego functioning is the real ticket to the sold-out stadium. Cheer for yourself rather than requiring it from others.

MICHAEL'S SOUL MISSION

To explore all facets of life and human behaviour.
To learn, love, create and evolve.
To learn more about self and love through relationships.
To access the full spectrum of my soul gifts and share them to entertain, inspire and teach about life.
To bring joy.

Guidance for today

We all have gifts. Discover your gifts as they are a perfect accompaniment for your designated soul missions. Be wise and discerning with how you employ your gifts or life can trip you up. Be grateful for every second you get to embrace and use them. Heal and heal some more so you can love your life and never take anything or anyone for granted. Avoid wasting your gifts. The world needs your talent and positive influence. If you are in the public eye, you have a great responsibility to model great being and living. Many youthful eyes are upon you looking for direction and inspiration. Are your 'transmissions' helping them to receive that which will move them forward on their journeys? Use your status to engage the better rather than the worse within those who cross your path—either in person or via other means.

THE CHOICE

Light (love) or dark (fear) can be chosen in any moment. Choose well for every thought, every emotion, has an accompanying action or reaction.

MICHAEL LANDON
Actor

If you don't like the self you're being, create a new one.

Every thought, word, deed has a corresponding effect, contributing not only to your life but to the energy of the whole. We do not exist in isolation, both in life and beyond life. There is a highly complex, divine system in place to support the enhancement of all of life. Be a great part of this system. Take care of your own paddock and help those around you to tend their pastures well—if it is in your power to do so. Responsibility first originates within self and then (if moved to do so) service can arise from the best self. For many individuals, service may be required just for self (for a time, even a lifetime), as there is much to release and transform before functioning as one's best. Be patient and compassionate with self and others to open to the potential of change. Life-enhancing change does not arise out of judgement, vilification or violence.

MICHAEL'S SOUL MISSION

To rise above circumstances to create new life.
To love.
To create.
To bring joy through entertainment.

Guidance for today

Conduct a regular review of self with kindness and no judgement as the foundation. Be honest with yourself. What makes you feel good about yourself and what do you need to change? Choose more of the life and vibe-enhancing qualities and less of the 'other'. We are all very familiar with the 'other'. Catch it, name it, release it, make the commitment to selecting better choices. Your heart will become more and more alive with the power of your goodness: a portal to magic and miracles.

THE CHOICE

Rise above your current circumstances no matter how amazing they are. There is always room for more growth, more pleasure and more service—a great trio for transformation! Remember you are an infinite, highly creative being. What will you do with this knowledge?

MICHAEL
Singer, Songwriter, Dancer

Live a colourful life—it should never be black and white.

Allow life to take you on many great adventures and lead you through many colourful experiences. Be open to the full spectrum of the rainbow. Avoid deciding that life should be this or that, for life knows better.

I never fully appreciated in life that inner joy is pure gold. In fact, nothing else compares. I sought much of what I was seeking externally, accumulating a great deal of what wasn't necessary. All the things that were seen were great ... I had everything! The things you couldn't see, some of the important things, were missing, and I didn't know where to find them. I had partially obscured my light with the distraction of material things. My grandiose choices were fun—a reward for my service and, at the same time, provided a great numbing escape for any inner turmoil that arose. My soul would have been more greatly nourished if I had used my wealth to heal my wounds. My accumulated treasures could then have brought a great, unbridled joy rather than a temporary fix.

Hindsight would have moved me to make seeking wholeness and joy a priority, and the foundation for greater living and more enjoyment of my gifts. All my experiences and all that I created would have been even more magnificent and loved by me—and felt even more deeply by those influenced by me—if I had been more connected to the power of inner love. Love is a powerful fuel to use in all your exploits. A love-inspired life is the greatest life, for it will be filled with profound healing and blessings and unlimited expression of soul gifts. I am absolutely amazed by what I achieved. I cannot even begin to imagine what I would have contributed to life with greater wholeness. Love ensures a complete life, with success and pleasure woven into each mission. Love has no limits and therefore neither do you.

MICHAEL'S SOUL MISSION

To be a force of creativity.
To demonstrate the power of creativity to transform.
To create joy and light through artistic expression.
To heal the soul.
To release karma.
To experience and express love.
To be a champion for the underprivileged and suffering.
To experience fun and light.
To learn to trust.
To teach the world to embrace the inner child.
To teach the world to create, sing and dance.
To demonstrate the power of artistry.
To forgive and give.

Guidance for today

Be the best you can be for all, self-included. Owning your worth and using this to step into your power provides a strong barrier against all that may seek to hurt you or exploit you in life. Your light is both a powerful medicine and powerful protection. Be open to the light in all your moments and all your days. It will heal you, soothe you and open you to the best within your missions in life. Seek to be a person who has no regrets or karma to absolve upon leaving Earth. Aim for a clear, clean slate and a great legacy.

THE CHOICE

Awaken from the dream that you are small, broken or wounded in any way. Heal yourself to create healing (and the potential of becoming whole) in your personal sphere and beyond. You and you alone have the wisdom for yourself—which is already within you. Claiming this truth would change much in the world as we too freely give away our power to something or someone we have deemed greater and, therefore, knowing best. Avoid allowing the noise of the world to interfere with your process. Create opportunities to quieten the noise for self and others wherever you can.

MOTHER TERESA
Nun, Missionary, Nobel Peace Prize Winner

Seed service into all that you do to manifest the highest conditions to actualise your missions.

Envision and feel into the world you would like to see. Thoughts and feelings create powerful energy and powerful magic. Energy creates movement in response to desire. The world needs this movement. Momentum behind change is the transformation those 'beyond this world, for this world' are infusing onto the planet right now. You are not alone. We hear and heed your call.

TERESA'S SOUL MISSIONS

To release inner suffering.
To ease the suffering of others.
To be and demonstrate love and compassion.
To create awareness and potential for change around poverty and suffering.
To serve.
To rise above Earthly circumstances and bring the energies of heaven to living.

Guidance for today

Compassion is key. Being willing to step inside someone else's shoes, even momentarily, makes a difference. Any individual who feels seen has an opportunity to connect with the love within, gain new awareness and consequently rise above current circumstances in some way. Every small change, even if seemingly imperceptible, is powerful. Compassion is the highest expression a soul can make in life. All personal missions are greatly amplified with compassion as the undercurrent.

THE CHOICE

Contribute to the love, peace and enlightenment
of self and the world ... for a greater world. Be open to
what the world around you requires. See and
act as called.

MUHAMMAD ALI
Boxer, Activist

Adopt 'I am the greatest' as your personal mission mantra.

Choosing to seek and be your greatest is not selfish or arrogant; it is your divine birthright. It is linked intrinsically to the success you desire and require within your soul missions. It is backing yourself even when no one else does. It is believing in yourself when the odds appear to be stacked against you. This is when you must rise the most. There is great power in always having your own back. This means you are owning yourself and your power. Believe in yourself and the gifts you have been given. This allows them to flourish and be best utilised for serving your life and assisting others to also serve life. All soul missions have elements of bettering the lives of others built into them. Belief in self is vital for others to believe in you: a powerful creative force opens for you with this combination. Believe your greatest life into existence.

MUHAMMAD'S SOUL MISSION

To rise above circumstances into personal greatness.
To believe in self.
To access personal power.
To be a voice for freedom.
To contribute to the whole.
To create.
To master.
To utilise talents to full potential.

Guidance for today

Meet your power by deflecting all that is employed to limit its potential. Your thoughts, beliefs about self and life, and the limiting judgements, opinions and expectations of others are good places to begin reflection and counteraction. Fight for your best life with peace in your heart and intuition as your guide.

THE CHOICE

Lean away from your weaknesses (safety) and into your greatness.
Your potential and power arise out of your willingness to seek your greatness. Life catches on quite quickly. There is great magic in intent. Your missions (and you) will thrive on your inner power.

NAPOLEON BONAPARTE
French Leader

Fight the good battle. Win the battle over self and use your light to wage war on darkness.

Allow your impact to be felt throughout the ages for reform and change. A legacy of darkness (if that is where you've channelled your energy) will follow you throughout time until it is karmically resolved via your efforts to do so. Create great karma so that negative, highly challenging experiences do not follow you into other lifetimes, hindering your days. Avoid cursing yourself by harming others.

Be and create joy as if your very life depends on it, for your most successful and content life does.

NAPOLEON'S SOUL MISSION

To explore, to discover.
To expand thinking.
To know darkness, to understand and seek light.

Guidance for today

Seeking the greatest version of yourself is a most desirous mission for all, as all beings are connected in thought, word and deed.
World change begins on an individual level. Millions of sparkles of light (you, dear reader, are one such light) create a cosmic cataclysm of spectacular magnificence.

THE CHOICE

Light or dark in any moment, both within
and via deed.

NATALIE WOOD
Actress

Cherish you as you are the gift you most desire and require.

Life is fleeting and enduring in the same breath, depending on how one feels in current circumstances. It is just one of the many paradoxes experienced in life; paradoxes which can define or destroy if we give our power away to anything or anyone. My worth was often not high enough to encourage trust in me and my intuition. Make your worth paramount because it is the foundation for all that you build and attract into your life. All you truly need is the power of you and then anything that accompanies that is icing on a very beautiful cake. Choose who you spend your time with (or your life with) well, as these choices infuse your mind with loving stories about you. If you don't choose well, the opposite happens: stories that are depleting, stifling and harmful at best. Negative relationships and the accompanying stories we adopt about ourselves leak our vital life force and limit our ability to create what our souls and missions require. Be the greatest version of yourself to draw in relationships that will assist you to step even more into the wonder of you. You and your most beautiful living require that. Release from your life those who cannot love you unconditionally. They cannot see you and thus can inadvertently obscure your own true vision. See all that surrounds you honestly. Change that which is not representative of the core of your being, or reflective of the inner missions that call to you as quiet, powerful whispers.

NATALIE'S SOUL MISSION

To learn discernment in relationships.
To connect with personal power.
To be and express beauty.
To create.
To entertain.
To love self and others.

Guidance for today

Meet your highest calibre of worth. Cultivate it moment to moment, day to day. Craft it as you would any special creation. Self-doubt is your enemy. It will keep you from owning and utilising your soul gifts—the ones that you need and the world also needs to experience.

THE CHOICE

It is better to be alone than to endure a toxic relationship. Set yourself free of settling for anything less than what is great for you. You are worth the best that life has to offer.

Avoid allowing the events of life to define you. Enjoy the clean slate and the opportunity to make new choices that the rising sun gifts us every day.

Much love and appreciation for the work you are doing (on you) that raises the vibration of the world, Natalie x

NEIL ARMSTRONG
Astronaut, Aeronautical Engineer, Aviator, Professor

The eagle has landed.

You have arrived. What a time of great celebration. Earth is blessed to have you and eagerly anticipates the full spectrum of your contribution in due course and in divine timing. Your mission has begun.

What will you do with your finite number of heartbeats? Enjoy my truth as fact: each step taken is a giant leap for humankind. And what will you do with this powerful knowledge? Use it to build faith and value into every small accomplishment. Do not lessen your living or dishonour yourself by expecting more of your achievements than is currently being revealed. You are exactly where life desires you to be. You just need to stay open to where your next steps desire to take you. Life is constant creation in motion. Keep up. Each small acknowledgment of success opens you up to another stage of your soul mission and then another. There is no endpoint while you are still breathing. You are infinite, your missions are infinite, Earth time is not. Look back on your life and know you made the most of every day.

NEIL'S SOUL MISSION

To explore new frontiers.
To use soul gifts to create, develop, investigate and design.
To create technology and knowledge for the betterment of humankind.
To value and engender peace within the world.
To open life to possibility within the unknown.

Guidance for today

The unmanaged, off-the-leash ego mind is really our only nemesis in life. Its ability to create fear (the great life limiter) is only ever going to attempt to prove to us what we can't become, can't achieve and can't enjoy within our soul missions. Make it your primary mission to free yourself from fear. Leap into the unknown without fear as a companion and you will journey beyond yourself, surpassing the original intent of many of your soul missions.

THE CHOICE

Look after your vessel—mind, body and soul—to
support your highest mission.
Make the choice to go beyond; be beyond.

NELSON MANDELA
South African President

Begin by freeing yourself and then be the invitation for others to free themselves. Freedom is contagious.

Living in freedom begins within each individual. Freedom arises with the release of limiting life-binding thoughts, attitudes and dispositions. Freedom is found on the other side of fear and all its expressions of limitation. One individual finding freedom (within), and then in life, inspires others to do the same via example. True leaders lead from the heart and demonstrate freedom (and all other desirous states) by modelling this first in their own living.

NELSON'S SOUL MISSION

To embrace peace within and transform others through its power and potential.
To promote inclusivity and equality.
To be a voice for change and evolutionary growth.
To encourage vision.
To invoke collective thinking and movement.
To create the idea of global people.

Guidance for today

Find your voice and use it well. Your voice matters and is a harbinger for greatness and change. Allow your voice to alchemise untruths into truths. Do not ever fear your truth as it provides the avenue for you to meet and embrace your freedom.

THE CHOICE

Choose love, truth and freedom ... or the stagnating impact of fear and limitation: personal gaol.

NICHOLAS I
Russian Tsar

Fight not, my friend, for your ego is your only real foe.
Befriend your greatest ally in life: the real you.

Making peace with self is the first and last lesson of life. All that falls in between is a representation of the strength of your inner peace. Peace is your power and the key to your potential. Know peace to know yourself. Any personal reaction is a gateway to discovering what stands between you and your peace. Make all decisions from a place of peace and your soul callings and accompanying missions will feel like they are designed for you, as they are—because you've heard and received them.

NICHOLAS'S SOUL MISSION

To know the excesses and pitfalls of functioning from and leading through fear and ego.
To lose control, to suffer, to fail, to struggle in life as motivation to connect with the light within and above.

Guidance for today

Fight only the battle within ... if not, war of your own making will consume you and play out in your external world.

THE CHOICE

Be ego-led or soul-led.
Illuminate the darkness within self and shine light where possible all around your sphere of influence. Individual growth and healing first, then assist others on their path, if guided to do so. If not, it is too easy to become distracted from our own healing work (which is our primary role) by focusing our attention outside of ourselves. This can become another form of addiction as it is taking us away from the work we need to do, hence numbing us to what is going on within. Live within you and radiate this essence outwards.

PATRICK SWAYZE
Actor, Dancer

All steps are part of your unique, perfectly choreographed dance.

Life will take you out or elevate you to dizzying heights based on your reaction to each and every circumstance and experience. Pause, breathe and receive the truth of each encounter. Ask, 'What is really going on here?' Awareness is key—it is our protector and a ticket to more of our potential and the lessening of unpleasantness standing in our way. Be in the light and return all that is not light for universal processing. The universe is equipped to handle anything and anyone. You don't have to do it all alone as it is often just too much. There are mysteries encoded within every interaction (both pleasant and unpleasant) that can teach us much about self, life and our place within it. Be a sleuth: understanding is power. Be intentional with your thoughts and actions and surround yourself with those who do likewise. The people you gather in life need to reflect the best of you. People that spend more time in the dark will not fuel your light. Let them be, freeing you to be radiant you. Life doesn't have to be a random and tumultuous experience if you stand in your wisdom, peace, integrity and power.

PATRICK'S SOUL MISSION

To explore and balance divine masculine and divine feminine energies.
To love and be loved unconditionally.
To work with my soulmate to transform and be transformed.
To bring a variety of potential male role models to life on the screen.
To dance through life, to move, to create, to live fully and exuberantly regardless of life circumstances.

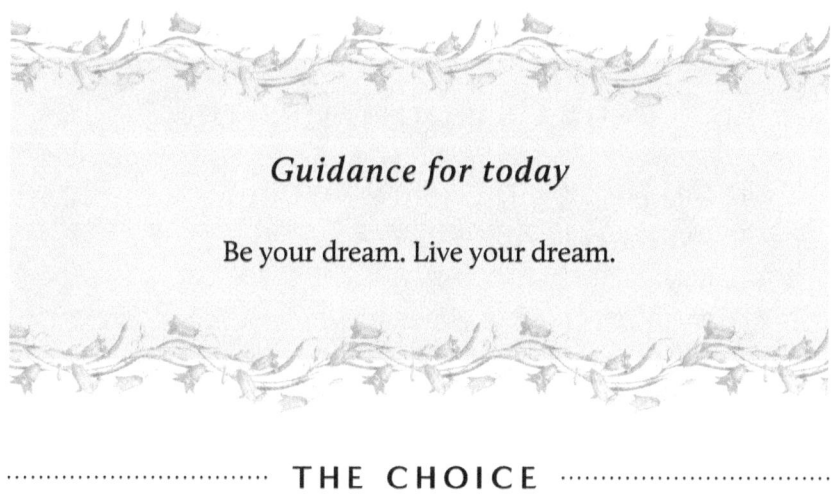

Guidance for today

Be your dream. Live your dream.

THE CHOICE

Be true to oneself or be consumed by life.
Dance to your own orchestra. You have unique moves to express.

PAULA YATES
Television Presenter, Writer

Life is both messy and magical. Be one with all of life—there is peace in that.

Embrace the opposites within life and learn to be all that you can be through all experiences. Life is the consummate teacher, as are the relationships that we draw into our world. There is a relationship and experience for every important lesson. We are not graded in life. Every experience is valuable. We are born as love, and we leave as love.

PAULA'S SOUL MISSION

To entertain.
To love and be loved.
To play.
To laugh and create laughter.
To create by exploring and utilising innate gifts.
To be and experience joy and fun.
To spread light.
To be an advocate for the choices and unique expressions available to women.

Guidance for today

Fighting against the currents of life makes for misery. Channel your energy into the good fight. Accept what is and at the same time proactively respond to any sense of unease before it becomes unbearably loud. The unease may originate from within—or flow in via the external world. Listen to the little nudges of inner wisdom. Our wisdom is constantly trying to guide us, lead us to pivot in a new direction, rethink a choice or consider an alternate decision. There is always hope; never give up on yourself or your dreams. Each desire and dream provides a unique breadcrumb trail for helping you to seek all that is also seeking you. Feeling called to your mission will lead you to your greatness and unlimited potential. You have a direct line with universal power and guidance—answer the call.

THE CHOICE

Never, ever give up on self or life. There is much to be achieved and enjoyed—the two are not mutually exclusive. Remember it is often darkest before the dawn. Hold on to hope, faith and trust as your greatest allies in all of your days.

POPE JOHN PAUL II

Build bridges and create riches based on faith, not fear.

Be led through life and all accompanying experiences through faith and love. Fear brings out the worst in humanity and all individuals. There is light and dark within all beings, even those who live on pedestals of goodness. Moment to moment, lean into your light (your love) and eventually the darkness within will be but a faint glimmer. Bliss can be an attainable state, not just something that exists in the ethers of heaven. Your darkness (a part of the collective lineage of humanity) will always be there to remind you of the need for your light. Be vigilant, alert to any negative lines of thinking or malaise that may be inadvertently drawing you away from your innate light and, at the same time, enjoy all the challenges and joys that life presents. Life is an education in the paradox of dark and light. Please trust that light always prevails even when it does not appear that way.

JOHN PAUL'S SOUL MISSION

To be a guide for leading towards the light.
To reconcile differences amongst people(s).
To ease suffering in self and others.
To teach the power of forgiveness.
To practise and embrace the power of faith.

Guidance for today

Follow your joy, go where it wants to take you without resistance. Love underpins your joy and extinguishes the darkness. The dark enjoys rearing its head (via the ego) at any time.
Ask daily:
Where can my joy take me on this day?
What would my joy have me do and say on this day?

THE CHOICE

Life is always shades of grey, capable of opening
to light or descending into the depths of darkness.
Make the choice, the demand on self to stand in your
light. Your inner peace (and her best friend, love) will
reward you greatly in life.

PRINCE PHILLIP
Duke of Edinburgh

*If you truly desire to see, and aspire to lead and transform,
go deeper, then deeper again.*

Much of life is open to interpretation and unfolds day to day according to one's engagement with a very personal reality. Although we are intertwined with many, the way we see and respond to life is unique to every individual. The most important work is on self. We can't do great things as a collective until all the elements (each being) heal the inner turmoil, face the illusions of the ego and become whole rather than a fragmented aspect of the potential whole. Whatever your current situation, station or role in life, approach everything from your inner world as that is where the truth, the freedom and the concurrent potential arises. We are 'unwell' as a species. We must rectify this because if not, we repeat 'inherited' patterns, thus continuing the same loop connecting us to illusion and limitation. Wake up, my friend. It only takes one moment, one truth, one awareness, one revelation at a time to meet the entirety of you. From this space, you contribute to new ways of being that have the potential of heralding and opening great paradigm shifts.

PHILLIP'S SOUL MISSION

To learn to access self within a powerful (limited) system and, in doing so, change, expand and up-level said system for the betterment of all.

Guidance for today

Connect with your light (and lightness and laughter), for it will show you the way. Be willing to shine light on all forms of darkness, beginning with the inner shadows.
Be serious about your purpose and mission, but paradoxically don't take anything too seriously.

THE CHOICE

Vision or avoidance.
Seeing, owning, and releasing all that is in the way of one's greatness and ensuing ability to serve.

QUEEN ELIZABETH I
Queen of England

Know your own mind, seek your own awakened wisdom and then share it for the advancement of all.

Birth does not have to be the defining factor in one's life. Rise above family norms, structures and patterns to create something new within your lineage. If not, unhelpful familial patterns can flow through to generation after generation. Recognise these intergenerational trends to release the (often subliminal) impact they can have on you and your life. Change begins with you, my friends.

What would you like to release from your ancestral imprint?

How would you like to open your lineage to more?

What could you choose to have, be and create that no one who has gone before you has envisioned?

Set great new intent for your current life and for those who follow in your brave footsteps. In today's world, mere survival is not the all-consuming issue in many parts of the world that it once was. Those living with great conditions need to use this fortunate status to improve the circumstances of others. Privilege comes with great responsibility. Use the extra space provided by states of freedom and improved life conditions to grow and evolve in unprecedented ways for self and others. Enhance the life of another and this act will bring forth much universal abundance for you.

ELIZABETH'S SOUL MISSION

To lead with consistency and adherence to personal moral codes.

To cohesively bring individuals together for a common purpose.
To explore the power of the individual within a patriarchal structure.
To find peace within, amidst external chaos.
To listen to the truth of self.
To express personal voice.
To establish personal boundaries.

Guidance for today

Lead your fellow beings into places few have ventured before. Expose others to new possibilities and your own life will expand in both expected and equally unexpected ways. Divine magic and miracle creation is your birthright.

THE CHOICE

Be for self and be for all.
Change yourself and you are changing the world, one awakened thought and one enhanced vibration at a time. Good living and being is beautifully catching.

QUEEN ELIZABETH II
Queen of England

God save the world, with the assistance of all.

Honour was my soul virtue. All that I did and all that I was ... was geared towards living a soul-led life with the ideal of bringing beings and nations along with me. Sometimes I did not know where I began and the job ended; both of us were irrevocably intertwined. It was a huge machine, a juggernaut, often with a life of its own. Sometimes I steered it; other times it steered me—such is human nature. Being so much a part of it all made it challenging to step outside to truly see a bigger picture. I hope to imbue those who come after me with that potential. I hope that just because something was always done a certain way that the possibility for change and transformation is not overlooked. Small steps towards newness will create powerful waves of change. The institution should not be a prison for its inhabitants. Freedom of expression and freedom to be individual and authentic needs to be the gentle new breeze flowing in for new life. The shadow aspects are requiring light. Light is what is called for moving forward. Royalty should hold life to the highest standards of love and compassion. At the same time, it should also be a symbol for hope, grandeur, beauty, grace and all things that are possible in life—with an underpinning value of equality, rather than the ego construct of superiority. No one needs to bow to another unless they feel so inclined out of respect or admiration; a title should not be synonymous with homage. Respect, trust and admiration are earned, not bestowed by birth or any other position of privilege.

ELIZABETH'S SOUL MISSION

To influence and elevate life to the highest calibre.
To unite souls for good.
To explore love, duty, honour and integrity.

Guidance for today

Aspire to be the absolute greatest version of yourself and life will conspire to help you to best lead you and others.

THE CHOICE

Be royal in all that you do and all that you are,
regardless of origin of birth.
There is potential royalty within all.

RAQUEL WELCH
Model, Actress

Live globally, dwell internally.

A beautiful thing about life on planet Earth right now is that many beings are beginning to grasp the connectedness of all things. We all ripple our own pond, which creates ripples in all the ponds of the world. Each thought, each deed, is stored in an Earthly memory bank and is used in some way in some time. Everything you are called to do for yourself and for those you love is, in effect, serving the whole. We are now all global citizens. Unrest in one part of the world infiltrates the souls and psyches of many. Some days, for no apparent reason, you may feel a sense of unease. Just know that some place or groups of individuals on the planet are requiring your prayers, your energy. Tune into this sense of unease (sensitive types know what I mean) and ask for universal assistance to channel your precious energy to where it can most serve. You will find the unease will lift. Unease, if it is not directly related to your current circumstances, is a call for action. The frequency that you emit is more powerful than you perceive. Open to greater possibilities for the use of your energy. Energy is timeless and knows no bounds.

RAQUEL'S SOUL MISSION

To express powerful female representations of beauty, strength and intelligence.
To challenge existing paradigms that define women and their roles.
To create and explore choice.
To be free to be.

Guidance for today

Reverse the program that indicates that taking care of yourself is selfish. Be the best you can be for self and then others. Powerful you transforms much of what ails in this world. Seek your wholeness and allow it to uplift and heal others.

THE CHOICE

Have your head buried in the sand or look up, look within and all around to truly see what is happening in the world—within and around you. Awaken. Find your niche, your purpose, your loves, and enjoy them passionately. Love your life and it will love you back.

REDDY
Actor

Seek inner fame and you will know true stardom.

Acknowledge and embrace the power of your charm and smile. Often, the simplest of gifts bestowed on us are the most powerful. Your mission this lifetime may be to just make others smile—there is great power in that. Ease any pressure to be or do what does not feel in alignment with you. Perhaps you have done enough this lifetime, or are still recovering from the last one, and now it's time to relax and enjoy the fruits of your labour. Perhaps it's time to retire from being or doing anything that does not light that inner fire. Don't get absorbed by a desire for grandiose outcomes. It's okay to dial it back, to go with the flow, to see what shows up and to just be who you feel like being. Maybe you've turned enough soil and it's time to receive the light to bring everything into bloom.

REDDY'S SOUL MISSION

To lean into light; to be led by light.
To explore the transformative power of fun and pleasure.
To love.
To create joy for self and others.

Guidance for today

There is a fine line to walk with any desire for success, and most definitely if there is a craving for stardom. Let your star rise in its own way and time without aiming for recognition, status, wealth or fame. These conditions are often a sign of ego-functioning and are non-enduring and unsustainable for inner peace and contentment in the long term. Aim for a slow burn rather than an immediate explosion.

THE CHOICE

Seek inner fortitude, worth, respect and love as opposed to seeking it from the fleeting 'external world' that is always more concerned with itself than you.

RETA SHAW
Actress

Be brave in life and true to yourself.

Our soul missions thrive through all expressions of love. I always found that no matter what my roles were in life, when I made choices that supported the nurturing of me all elements of my soul missions thrived. A nourished soul is a more effective and loving soul.

Our best life is enhanced by great choices. Sometimes there is so much choice and so much information and accompanying expectations that we can become overwhelmed. Listen to advice but be discerning, knowing what is true for you.

Sleep was an extremely important aspect of my soul care and is an area that creates duress if we don't tie in with current ideals. There are many current theories on sleep. Sleep is a great healer. It is a vitally important time for us to connect with our guidance and rest into the power of our dreams because the ego and the demands of the day are quiet for the night. Sleep gives us a rest from being ourselves. We get to take the night off. Sleep is our primary source of restoration. No one ever questions the benefits of sleep, however, all the emphasis on its importance can create unnecessary stress. If your sleep patterns do not currently follow 'desired' patterns and are in fact far from the norm, avoid allowing this to create unease and judgement. After you have done everything you can to ensure a good night's sleep, relax into the ebbs and flows and patterns of it. Your sleep patterns will change as you change and will be vastly different from decade to decade. Avoid creating sleep anxiety by deciding your sleep has to be a certain type or for a certain length of time each night. Look at how you function in your waking hours to determine the effectiveness of your sleep. Trust in your body and your being—accepting that no two nights of sleep may be the same. Sometimes you may need to be in bed at 8.00 pm and sleep for nine hours. Other nights, you may be asleep at 10.00 pm and ready for action at 4.00 am. Other nights, your genius may arrive at 2:30 am and require some action. Use how you are feeling as a gauge for how you are sleeping. Most importantly, release judgement around what is occurring. Your best sleep needs your peace and relaxation.

RETA'S SOUL MISSION

To embody and express female diversity.
To create to entertain and promote awareness of possibility for women.
To love.
To contribute and serve.
To comfort and nurture.

Guidance for today

Care for yourself mentally, physically, emotionally and spiritually in all of your days. Trust that your needs vary as you vary, and act accordingly. Give yourself permission to support yourself in all ways to support all your days. Your personal care and personal love are essential for your highest service towards self and your accompanying missions.

THE CHOICE

Follow your own compass when navigating choices. There are many strong compasses out there. Make sure your own is the strongest and kept in working order. Life at this time (more than ever) requires an excellent navigation system. It is within you, always.

Love, Reta x

RICHARD THE LIONHEART
King of England

Embrace your inner lion or lioness, remembering that your heart knows no bounds—only those you impose on self.

Start your life, don't wait for it. There is much to be done, much to achieve and much to be. Life is far shorter than you perceive it to be. Make each day count by treating each day as a complete life in itself. It is completely amazing what great deeds can be achieved in a day. Imagine the power of your lifetime missions if each day was held as a sacred opportunity for growth and achievement. Honour each new day as the sun rises, setting great intentions and reflect on your choices and moments of success and gratitude upon its completion. Rest, sleep, renew, restore and bravely step into the next day and the next. Remember why you have come. Remember who you are; it is far greater than you currently see or know. You will meet all the great aspects of your being if you continue on this path of understanding yourself and your place in the grand scheme of life.

RICHARD'S SOUL MISSION

To lead self and others.
To embrace power and bravery.
To leave a legacy of light and strength.
To seek knowledge and adventure.
To create.

Guidance for today

Did you enjoy yesterday? If so, what will you open to more of for creating even more abundance of all things good, enjoyable and successful? If not, what do you need to change right now? Your demands on self are extremely powerful weapons against limitation of all kinds. Take command of your life. Lead it well and motivate the action states of others by your example.

THE CHOICE

Stand tall. Feel into this. Let your bravery, love and presence lead your life.

ROALD DAHL
Author

Bring the healing power of joy and laughter to the world through your endeavours.

Every soul has a mission; some have several. Your mission(s) will find you if you surround your life with what brings you love and with what resonates with the essence of the truth of your being. Sway from the truth of yourself and you'll sway from your purpose. It can be challenging to 'locate' one's truth as it will not be the same as anyone else's. Your truths pertain to your unfolding as a being. They are reflected in the ways you utilise your inner knowledge to transform yourself to support your core mission(s). Each decade will reveal new truths and accompanying detours in your life trajectory. Let life take you. Do not resist who you need to be, what you need to do and where you need to go. Your blueprint guide is within you and contains all that you require for successfully activating your missions. All that is needed to connect with this inner guidance is for you to make the commitment to be the very best version of you in as many ways—in as many of your days—as possible. Know that some days you will veer off-path and be an obnoxious, self-serving annoyance to self and others—and that is okay, perhaps even necessary for showing you who you want to be and don't want to be. You will feel good when you are being authentic and will draw this in more and more when committing to serving self and others to the best of your innate ability.

ROALD'S SOUL MISSION

To create a culture of questioning and challenging the status quo.
To invoke the power of humour and laughter.
To teach about the shades within humanity.
To develop a love of and understanding of the power of the imagination.
To invoke the healing possibilities of visualisation and fantasy.
To teach about love and compassion.
To experience love through creation.
To promote a love and appreciation of the power of the written word.
To encourage people to embrace the power of frivolity in life.
To use personal influence to create positive change.

Guidance for today

Create the you that you dream of becoming. Create the life you dream of creating.

THE CHOICE

Reflect on where you currently stand on the continuum of your magnificence. Commit to seeking yourself and your highest soul calling with great fervour, love in your heart and a twinkle in your eyes. True missions are infused with love, laughter and an abundance of all kinds of wonderful. Our missions are divine and infused with cosmically aligned gifts. Enjoy unwrapping your gifts; aren't they simply exquisite and packaged so beautifully?

ROBERT GUILLAUME
Actor

Life as you've known it is dissipating; your new chapter is alchemising into being.

There is much transformation occurring in life during these times. Many are in different stages of metamorphosis. Be patient with self and others. When you emerge, really spread your wings. Don't hold back. Let your wings inspire others to unveil their most spectacular selves. Open your wings and let your dreams and desires draw towards you, for you have waited long enough. It is now time to receive the fullness of your life—a life filled with adventure and forays into the unexpected, spontaneous and unknown. Doesn't even just reading about possibility feel different in your soul? You know it to be true. There is so much more waiting for you to meet.

Third-dimensional living has been challenging as it revolves around fear, lack, unrealised dreams, control, apathy and hopelessness for many. Most of you are tired of this way of being. You no longer see its value or relevance and are seeking more, even if this is not fully realised yet. This is all part of the awakening process. The current despondency is creating the inner frustration necessary for the demand on self and life for more. It is time to move into the space of life being mysterious, mystical and magical. Your soul desires to enter the realm of miracles, a place where there is light and spark within you. You are bored with the old way of living; you'd rather sleep or withdraw than engage with it anymore. You are done with monotony. Celebrate this realisation and the concurrent opening to greater streams of light flowing into you and your reality. Your soul missions are about to accelerate. Enjoy magical moments of, 'I didn't see that coming!' You couldn't because you haven't lived this way before. Once it begins, there is no turning back and you will never desire to do so because life is about to become much more fun and meaningful. Prepare to meet your passion, possibly many of them!

ROBERT'S SOUL MISSION

To explore freedom and choice.
To use humour to elevate living.
To create.
To entertain.
To find passion and purpose and express this for the enjoyment of all.

Guidance for today

Prepare to leave the mundane behind. Your soul desires to be ignited and your miracles unleashed—as per Jane's previous book! You don't need to know what that's going to look like. You just need a willingness and desire for such a transition so you can move into a new way of being, receiving and serving life.

THE CHOICE

Not all beings will move out of third-dimensional living and that is their choice, just as you are choosing to go beyond this space. You have overstayed but many will remain. Your challenge is to raise your vibration in all your days despite what those around you are doing and being. If you have read Jane's previous books, you will already know how to do this. Be vigilant, stay the course. Your rewards and pleasure in this new world will be greater than you can imagine.

ROBERT THE BRUCE
King of Scots

Find the light warrior within and break free of the walls you've erected to avoid your highest destiny.

Leadership of the future will be very different to that of the past: more resonant with moving into a new Earth frequency. Leadership will not be based on control, greed, coercion, overt displays of strength, narcissistic violent undertones or bought with wealth. Leaders of the future will inspire and be for, and connected to all of humanity with equality, peace, human consciousness and evolution as dominant undercurrents. Leaders will create leaders, with en masse awakenings amongst beings who connect to the same universal source of light. Oneness, rather than separation, is the leadership paradigm of the future. Each being who learns to lead self (claiming personal sovereignty and light) greatly influences the leadership potential within others.

ROBERT'S SOUL MISSION

To explore the concept of freedom.
To wage war on the darkness within.
To lead freedom movements.
To fight oppression.
To atone for the misuse of power.
To learn how to lead self and others.

Guidance for today

Lose the desire to fight all that is out of your control. Use your light to influence what can be influenced in your sphere. Selectively lead. Conserve your energy and share your truth only when it does not fall on deaf ears. Be yourself and your audience will find and see you. Lead by example in the way that is inspiring for you. Deflect the energy of the naysayers. Allow them to open to truth and light on their own timeline. They see you, hear you and are subtlety transformed by your presence and energy more than you know—and it's not for you to know. How your energy is felt, and the way it alchemises unconsciousness into greater openings for awareness to drop in, is incredible. How other beings respond is not your concern. Take your energy away from focusing on results outside of you as tuning into the potential outcomes for others is a great drain on your vital energy reserves. Your energy is for doing what you are called to do, no more and no less; the effect on the world via your presence is for the world to experience outside of you.

THE CHOICE

Live with purpose. A purposeful life is a well-lived, well-loved life. Your mission is like no other, just as it should be and is so for all.

ROBIN WILLIAMS
Actor, Comedian

Replace fear with fun and frivolity.

Be generous with your light and laughter because your joy is a superpower. Super you has a spectacular superhero cape. Can you picture it? Allow it to trail behind you everywhere. Regularly remind the world of the super being you truly are! As you know, this world requires superheroes. We have always required heroes and warriors for the light, but we need them now more than ever because a new age is calling. Light is breaking on Earth for all her creatures, great and small. Play your part. Serve self and life to the highest calibre. Give what you can, to receive what you can.

ROBIN'S SOUL MISSION

To spread light through laughter.
To entertain and amuse.
To transmute lower vibrational energies.
To open the masses to light and love.
To create, to play, to imagine.
To explore the unknown.
To transform suffering into wisdom and light.

Guidance for today

My question: Robin, how did you get to be so funny?
His answer: Be authentic and light. Don't take life seriously. Treat it like the most joyful, creative and imaginative childhood game possible. Laugh in the face of everything, especially darkness. The dark fears laughter, joy and frivolity because it is extinguished by it. Life is actually very funny! Unbalanced people (definition open to interpretation) are funny because they have forgotten who they truly are—beings of vast greatness. There is a funny side to much of what life throws our way if we are willing to receive it. Being myself, owning all the places I knew did not fit the norm connected me with the depths of my humour, which became a daily surprise and antidote for inner despair. The more conscious and lighter you become, the funnier you become. I am looking forward to Earth becoming The Laughing Planet. That is my vision and I'm holding onto it.

THE CHOICE

Return all that is not light to the universe, to the heavens (wherever your faith exists) to be transmuted into that which is for the highest good. Allow light to prevail, moment to moment through your choices, thoughts, words and attitudes. Note to self (and for you): it all begins with thought.

ROGER MOORE
Actor

Be a part of something larger than yourself to expand more fully into your greatest self and the accompanying largesse of life.

One of the added benefits of accessing one's soul gifts is that it opens new doors that are closed unless there is a conscious choice to best utilise soul talents. Each soul has gifts and interests that predispose each to greatness and heightened opportunities if acted upon. Ignore your gifts at your own detriment.

Each time we develop a talent, our life changes; the people we associate with in relation to our gifts change, as do the things we get to experience. I learned much about myself, others and life by using my acting ability. My creative abilities served me well, allowing me to expand into new arenas, meet inspirational people to support my own growth and bring joy to self and many. My life involved the power and abundance of giving and receiving and showing up for my gifts.

ROGER'S SOUL MISSION

To love.
To learn about self through relationships.
To act for pleasure and entertainment.
To balance giving and receiving.
To use gifts to serve and thus contribute to the whole.
To access wisdom.
To open up to mentors.

Guidance for today

Being around greatness and like-minded souls makes us reach for more—within ourselves and in life. Move in new circles. Indulge in new interests. Find as many ways as you can to discover your soul gifts. Try something new to meet something new within you. Seek something that appears larger than you and has great appeal; diligently work towards it one moment, one day at a time.

THE CHOICE

Sometimes there appears to be no choice. Relax. The soul mission calling is so great that life creates upon itself. Resistance is futile and akin to forcing oneself to stop breathing.

SAINT FRANCIS OF ASSISI
Italian Mystic

Make your life magical and mystical to feel an aliveness within and an opening to potential and possibility.

Embrace the mysterious. There is much to understand about yourself and life through what you don't know, see or understand.

Stay open to learning. Be curious in all of your days. Avoid jumping to conclusions. Know that everything is subjective. There are always many layers within one truth, including within your own. Always ask, 'What else is here for me to know?' See everything as an interesting point of view rather than an impermeable or static state. No being, organisation, institution or authority ever has all the answers, especially if they imply that they do. You have the guidance book for your life encoded within you. Embrace your inner mystic to unlock the mystery of you. Imagine a world where every being had access to their own wisdom, their own unique blueprint for enhancing life for self and others. That is the world I hope to see. Hold this vision with me now. Your missions are all divine. Do what it takes to accept and actualise them.

ST FRANCIS'S SOUL MISSION

To awaken self and others to mysticism.
To know and teach spiritual truths.
To understand life and how it works best.
To create through love.

Guidance for today

Invoke your star power, that place within you that is not tainted by the less than favourable experiences in life or by some of the unpleasant collective energies. Surround yourself in the protective and elevating energies of the stars. Draw this universal energy down into and around your body to raise your vibration to most effectively meet your missions. What is above is also within you. Remember your source, your starry origins. You are far more than just this Earthly life. Allow the stars to guide you home to you. Connect and remember.

THE CHOICE

Be a mystic, moving beyond the intellect to connect with your true Earthly potential—infused with cosmic influence. Surrender to oneness and to the guidance available within the sacred.

SEAN CONNERY
Actor

As you open, life opens.

Life is a reciprocal dance. The things you desire don't come your way unless there is the willingness to receive them in your heart. Many individuals (I know you're not one of them) spend much of life blocking their good as they unconsciously anticipate the worst or fear failure. What is failure anyway, if not a limited ego perception based on illusion? Find freedom from failure and enjoy much blissful risk-taking—or life-opening, as I view it. Laugh in the face of 'failure fear'.

Life is quite simple if we allow it to be so. Open up to what you desire. Make the creative space for something new and wondrous to flow in. Seek wonder and the mysterious as this is where the magic and miracles abound. Anything known does not contain the element of uncertainty from which possibility can arise. Pack your bags (both literally and figuratively) and head off somewhere tangible or even somewhere imaginary as a doorway to more. Where would your heart have you go? Relax into your awareness; you do not need to fear your choices. Engage in all of life until you find the places you would most like to land that best allow you to enjoy and share your gifts and light. Observation of all facets of life is great, but eventually, to truly live, you must dip your toes in many ponds, walk onto many playing fields and climb many mountains to reach great pinnacles. Your soul missions are designed for you and with you to create a bountiful life. Follow your heart to meet your missions.

SEAN'S SOUL MISSION

To follow the heart.
To experience abundance of all kinds.
To lean into the unknown.
To take calculated, conscious risks to live an expansive life.
To seek fun and adventure.
To create movies to awaken possibility and desire.
To live free of ego coercion.

Guidance for today

Make the decision to love and engage in your life rather than fear it. You are no bystander. You deserve to be centre stage, starring in your life. Be so focused on your living that you are not impacted by the choices of others or lessened by the ugly beast of comparison. Be cool my friends. You've got this. Stay present in today, one confident step after another. Before you know it, you will have blazed a trail that you can look back on with pride. I look back on life and smile. I lived well, so I died even better. I wish the same for you. I am beyond this world, but I am also for this world. As are you.

THE CHOICE

You are here, so go forth and live by soaking up all manner of experiences.
There is no other choice. Your mission is to live your best life: being, doing and going wherever life takes you on this wild ride towards the greatest expression of you. Evolution of the global collective asks this of us all.

SHAKTI GAWAIN
Inspirational Author

The universe will reward you for taking risks on its behalf.

Commit to learning to be true to yourself and this will predispose you to the creation of inner peace and a natural drawing in of all that you require for your most successful living and accompanying soul missions. The universe is awaiting your connection, for it desires to guide you and gift to you beyond what you may be able to presently imagine.

Life is about leading you towards discovering your own inner genius—a 'genius' for making your living both a delight and a force for creating transformation within others.

We are all moving forwards as a species and what impacts one, impacts many. There is no place for stagnation. Evolution currently requires our greatest collective momentum.

We find our soul dispositions and innate gifts by connecting with our true essence which can often be found within the polar opposites of the popular opinion and popular choices around us.

Conformity, whilst safe and comfortable, will only give you a predictable life, not one filled with intrigue, great adventure, new frontiers and wonder. Open the channel for the wisdom contained within you to lead your life. Avoid wanting to duplicate someone else's life as it is not the one chosen by you at a soul level. Trusting and being yourself makes your soul missions find you, often with miraculous ease. You do not need to concern yourself with how things are going to be revealed for you; instead, focus on being a clear channel and vibrational match for your desires. What you desire is actually spirit nudging you in directions for supporting your soul work and mission. Listen to these whispers and follow your heart to all the beautiful experiences and destinations planned for you.

SHAKTI'S SOUL MISSION

To awaken self and others to how life really works.
To use the power of intention and awareness for manifestation.
To harness the power of the mind for creative visualisation.
To assist others to align with their soul potential, gifts and missions.

Guidance for today

Follow your inner guidance to feel aligned with your soul and its accompanying missions for this incarnation. In doing so, you will feel energetically beautiful and connected to the power of the cosmos. There is much joy to be experienced when we are aligned with our purpose. Life has meaning and a sense of ease. Plug into infinite universal potential for actualising your purpose and passion. This is true living. Light the way in your world and simultaneously be a beacon for others.

THE CHOICE

Safe and predictable living or unknown and expansive living.

SHIRLEY TEMPLE
Actress, Singer, Dancer, Diplomat

Believe not what the world will say about you. Your heart is your true guide and closest ally.

Seek your inner strength as you will need it in great amounts to successfully navigate your missions. The 'less than light' forces on the planet will tell you that you are not enough, are unworthy of success and are, in fact, wasting your time trying to rise above your current station or in striving to make a difference in the world. Luckily, none of this is true. Please do not believe anyone including the voice of your ego or the whispers of an ancestral lineage that paints any picture that does support the unlimited artistic canvas that should represent your life. Be impervious to the judgements and limitations that may come along to influence your missions. Listen to the voice of truth within you—you will know it by its positive, supportive, expansive approach. Giving in to society-fuelled doubt or collective despair is not supportive of your missions.

SHIRLEY'S SOUL MISSION

To understand and apply universal laws of creation.
To connect with flow.
To transform self and circumstances.
To be an agent for love and peace.
To create.
To bring joy through entertainment.

Guidance for today

In all your days, be aware of who and what lifts you up and who and what depletes you. Your energy is everything as it infuses your thoughts, beliefs and emotions with like, moment to moment.

THE CHOICE

You are precious. Treat yourself accordingly and avoid individuals and experiences that do not have your back. Take comfort in knowing that every day the universe has your back. You are guided, you are loved. Receive this truth and wrap it around you as a cosy, uplifting blanket.

SIDNEY POITIER
Actor, Film Director, Diplomat

*Let your body be a star in this lifetime so you
can do your best work.*

Avoid allowing your body (via ego manipulations) to steal your peace. Let your body do its thing as a master healer and regenerator without sacrificing its capacity for wellbeing by listening to the ego commentary. The ego will seek to alert you (and control you) by getting you to focus on everything that is possibly wrong with your body instead of focusing on what is absolutely right about it.

Life is really a journey from the ego-self back to the higher-self, and from diseased thinking to free, loving, unlimited thinking. Your body produces millions of new cells every day. It is programmed to regenerate itself and to seek wellness every day. Your job is to support this regeneration with healthy, life-enhancing thoughts and clean-living choices. Trust your body, trust you. Free yourself from the great hook the ego uses to capture your attention and take you down the route of fear-based thinking. Every time you feel something different or even unpleasant in your body, seek to negate the ego's attempts to take you to the wrongness of the experience. Often, the greatest healing taking place does not feel pleasant. As the body unearths, processes and releases old toxins and pathogens, you will feel a few bumps and groans along the way. Your job is to love your body (and yourself) to support wellness. Worrying about your body hinders wellness and distracts you from your life missions (an ego endgame), whereas trust and gentle loving thoughts expedite healing and life potential. Avoid allowing the ego to take your power and make you feel weak and malleable by convincing you that you are unwell and deteriorating. Instead, design how you want your body to look and feel via loving, powerful thoughts. You are the powerful being creating your body; own this life-enhancing truth. Your cells respond to your thoughts, so program them well for vitality and health. Work to build a strong mind and thus build a strong body.

SIDNEY'S SOUL MISSION

To move from ego self to higher self.
To release fear and seek love.
To create to entertain and educate.
To seek and provide joy.
To develop mastery and excellence using innate gifts.
To promote peace.
To support the evolution of greatness.
To promote freedom, diversity and acceptance.
To open doors for respect and race equality.

Guidance for today

For many, the body is the final frontier of ego control because it knows how to tap into fear around health as it is a dominant collective theme. Awareness is freedom; freedom to be something and do something different. Now that you are out from under the control of the ego (via the body), what will you choose with all your regained peace and power?

You are free to be. You can now show up for your greatest missions and, most importantly, enjoy them! Bodily health is a divine birthright. Claim it now.

THE CHOICE

Trust in your body and its healing potential. Make peace with your body. Know that you are not your body (or your thoughts about it) but the powerful being behind both. Reclaim your throne, your power. Take charge and reign well over your ego. Make it your subject, not the other way around. Eventually, you may even be blessed enough for it to leave your kingdom for good, or at least become a silent servant. Make the choice to exile your ego.

SOPHIA LOREN
Actress

The soul endures, the body is a lifetime gift: keep things in perspective.

Avoid over-identifying with the body. It is not in charge of you. It does not get to determine how you feel, despite how it may be 'feeling'. Do not make your happiness, your worth or your power dependent on what your body looks like or feels like on any given day or at any life stage. It is not a reflection of your soul. The care you take of your body may or may not be reflected in its external appearance or internal wellness. Bodies often do things of their own volition without our full understanding. Your body is for fun and for moving about doing the things you love to do. Dress it up, adorn it, pamper it, enjoy it, but do not make it more significant than you or a determiner of your value. The value is within the being, your essence, your purpose and your missions. Society is too body-conscious, and this excludes the millions of beings who don't fit the current youthful, smooth, thin, age-defying (unrealistic, airbrushed or adulterated) gold standard for bodies and appearances. Allow your light to be fully seen and expressed by losing the vibration-lowering versions of self-judgement that can too easily creep into your days. Allow your body to enjoy the full potential of its vitality and wellbeing by directing positive thoughts its way.

SOPHIA'S SOUL MISSION

To create.
To design.
To become self-aware and life-aware.

To elevate self and others through entertainment.
To express grace.
To love.
To be free.
To be inspired and to be an inspiration.

Guidance for today

Keep body and soul in perspective. Too much thought power is wasted on bodily concerns that affect one's inner worth. Self-worth impacts our choices and influences what we are willing to receive, be and do in life. Know you are worthy. Show up for your life regardless of your shape and size. Present and care for your body for your pleasure (to the best of your ability) and then get on with things.

How you wear your hair or what adornments you choose today are for fun and not to use as an inauthentic representation of you. The great depths and true beauty of you cannot be contained within limited body expressions.

THE CHOICE

Know that your body is only a tiny aspect of you. You are an infinite, highly creative being. You are sacred. Act accordingly.

TENNESSEE WILLIAMS
Playwright, Screenwriter

Support the dream whilst the dream is unfolding.

Many of us see only brief glimpses of our potential and accompanying dreams at various stages throughout our lives. This is a part of the grand design of things. The system is not flawed. We inadvertently cause ourselves duress or push our dreams away by desiring too much too soon. Support all stages of your missions by working diligently and infusing kindness and personal growth into all thought and action. Patience is key. Our greatest dreams require time to weave into our reality. There is a magic that needs to flow within us and towards us to bring the grandest of our dreams to life. The universe has much to accomplish on our behalf to help us meet the magic required for our soul missions. This is sacred, very powerful work on our behalf and on the universe's behalf. We are mutual co-creative collaborators of the highest degree. Remember your divinity is the essence of your life.

TENNESSEE'S SOUL MISSION

To educate, inspire and entertain through the power of word and screen.
To create.
To seek magic.
To transform self.
To write desired life into reality.
To be and invoke kindness.

Guidance for today

Find the light within all things (including self) to become a hallowed container for magic and miracles to flow within. Value each chapter in life. There is no fun in skipping straight to the end.

THE CHOICE

Light up your life with beauty in the mind, tenderness in the heart and love in your work every day ... and hold no set outcome. Stay open to what you don't yet know and haven't yet become.

THOMAS EDISON
Inventor

Light the way for others and, therefore, illuminate more of your own path.

Dream new things into existence. See what 'isn't' and set about to create it. Stretch your mind to open up, work and function for you in new, challenging ways. The managed mind knows no bounds; use it to imagine and manifest well. Each creation has a domino effect, propelling new possibilities into existence. Make creation front and centre of your existence. Take note of all the creative acts that you perform in a day that may have gone unnoticed to acknowledge and therefore catalyse your creative potential. Each choice made is an act of creation. What are you creating with your choices? How did your choices benefit you today? How did your choices benefit your loved ones today? How did your choices enhance the world today?

THOMAS'S SOUL MISSION

To create and invent for joy and for the enhancement of life.
To stretch the boundaries of impossibility.
To harness the power of thought and imagination.
To be a beacon of potential in human evolutionary processes.
To master and utilise Earth's materials and gifts to serve life.
To open up to divine creative channels.

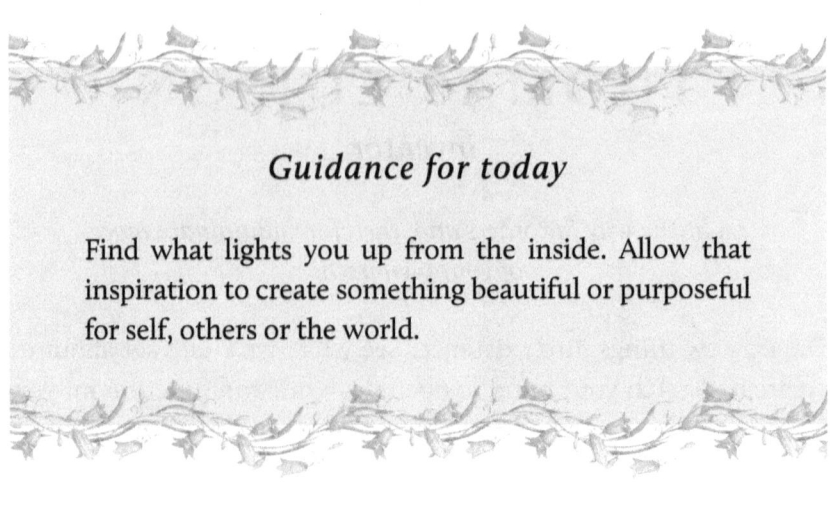

Guidance for today

Find what lights you up from the inside. Allow that inspiration to create something beautiful or purposeful for self, others or the world.

THE CHOICE

Be alive by living with possibility and exploring your potential. Expand into the greatest expression of you whenever possible.

THOMAS HARDY
Novelist, Poet

Surround yourself in an ever-blooming hedge of light.

If you decide to make fun, joy and enthusiasm the centrepiece of your life, then your missions will roll along beside you with a higher likelihood of effortless ease.

How you feel on the inside is always the most important. The action stuff comes second. Do the 'doing' when your heart is really in it, and you will create with aplomb and enjoy accompanying satisfying results.

THOMAS'S SOUL MISSIONS

To rise above conditions and create anew.
To change self and surrounding experiences.
To create awareness through the power of the written word.
To express and create.
To participate in social reform.
To develop consciousness and awareness of universal laws.

Guidance for today

Give yourself permission to protect yourself from certain aspects of life for participating most fully in your own soul missions. Not everything is for you or concerns you. Focus your attention and energy where you feel most deeply called to travel. Avoid spreading yourself too thin and thus weakening the energetic and personal impact you have the potential to make. I surrounded my home in a 'protective' hedge of trees which was great, but what I was really seeking was access to more protective, life-enhancing light. Find your light, be nurtured by it and radiate it well. Life loves light.

THE CHOICE

Lean into love of yourself. Lean into love of your life. Contribute as desired from the greatest, most content version of you and your life will be a creative masterpiece in the making.

TONY GREIG
Cricket Captain, Commentator

Give your heart and hands to your passions and they will take you on an unparalleled life journey.

Places have energy. Just as there is much coming up for individuals to heal at this time, many physical locations are requiring energy clearings and shifts. The old, even ancient, energies are rising to be released and remembered. There is much movement amongst the light workers on the planet as many beings are simultaneously gifted with the ability to shift energies within locations and to also receive the healing, awakening energies contained within certain places. If it is in your power to do so, go where you are called. There is something there for you that's energetic in nature that you require on some level for the next stages of your journey. There is a beingness that is desiring to come forth within you. This memory surfaces through a portal, a ley line configuration or a rock or crystalline structure that is calling to you via the Earth, or an energy associated with a particular geographical location. Tune into the vibration and the essence of places that call to you and light you up. There is a healing light code, or an energetic transmission that desires to come through for you to support you at this time for the next transformative evolution of you. Land sites and locations have power, absorb what is just for you, when it is for you.

TONY'S SOUL MISSION

To use gifts to create phenomenal life.
To be an authentic expression of self.
To explore and learn from global living.

To create a love of sport and movement.
To experience the energy of Earth, utilising it for healing and transformation.

Guidance for today

Love what you do and then explore and travel with your work or interests. Build travel and exploration into your living. There is much to learn, see, experience and unlock within you as you journey into each new place. If you remain stationary, the universe finds it more challenging to bring to you or reveal to you the vast array of all that it desires to gift you. There are people and destinations all over the globe that have much to teach you. Move people, particularly out of any self-imposed boxes. Movement of any kind is synonymous with moving forward and opening up to more of you and more of life.

THE CHOICE

Be the captain and commentator of your own life. Own self and life. Live purposefully and with great enthusiasm for all that you do and all that you are. Stand tall and allow the world around to feel your presence.

URSULA
Actress

You are a treasure map. Your journey in life and guiding mission is to find the gold encoded within you and share this with others.

Meet you, the real you, not the version that is a product of cultural and familial conditioning. She or he is a complex being. Know oneself with all inherent intricacies and accompanying secrets for unveiling soul-supportive, mission-enhancing, innate gifts. Life on Earth requires all our unique gifts for moving into a new age. Our gifts enable us to be alchemists, combining our power and skills for a transformative potential not witnessed for eons.

URSULA'S SOUL MISSION

To learn to love self and life and apply this to all experiences.
To embody the divine feminine and divine masculine.
To be an expression of beauty and possibility.
To empower women.

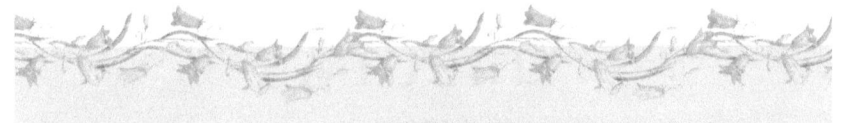

Guidance for today

Believe in the goodness, the magic and the potential in others. Avoid focusing on what is not working if your desire is to see more of what can work. Realise the power of your 'expectation'—a power never to be used lightly.

THE CHOICE

Be free of the inner plaintive and protagonist to meet the full cast and creative team behind your desired reality—the reality where you star and take the lead in your soul missions. The inner plaintive and protagonist have a cancelling effect on the 'star', hence why many individuals feel they take one step forward and two steps back. Tip the scales in favour of the best you and your best life. Consistency is a true superpower.

VIVIEN LEIGH
Actress

There is something just so right about you. Allow this truth to permeate your very essence.

The universe will always conspire with great benevolent forces to bring you home to yourself.

The ego, the scared part of you, is adept at finding your insecurities, guilt, shame and any other form of fear. It has your code, your number, and knows how to move you away from your true self via one carefully curated, niggling, negative emotion at a time. It is great at making things that aren't about you, about you. It wants to keep you small (and safe) no matter how uncomfortable and limiting that is for you. That is its job. You, however, don't need to be employed by it. You are your own boss. Change the chapter of the story the ego is unveiling for you into one that holds kindness and compassion for you. Turn to a vibrant, fresh new page. Move away from the usual culprits it captures—those encouraging you to believe you've done something wrong (in some way) or do not deserve your current peace and contentment. Breathe deeply. Connect with your inner guidance and ask, 'What is really going on here?' In this way, we use our self-doubt or any other uncomfortable reaction as a point of entry to uncover a truth. The truth will exist alongside the fearful ego, that is, the truth the ego wishes to conceal from you as it senses it will lose its grip and eventually dissipate. Remember it wants to survive at all costs. You are within your rights to assist its demise and move into higher-self presence and functioning.

VIVIEN'S SOUL MISSION

To immerse oneself in the complexities of human nature for learning about self and life.
To explore and represent diverse, powerful female roles.
To explore love in its various guises through creativity.

Guidance for today

After a difficult ego 'attack', reflect on why it may have been especially strong at this time. Were you tired, overwhelmed or recently triggered? Were your boundaries or energies compromised? Had you lowered your vibration? Had you moved out of your heart and into your head? Did you lose faith or believe in something non-supportive or true about you? Attempt to ascertain what made you vulnerable (to the ego) to gain greater freedom from it in future scenarios.

THE CHOICE

There would be such freedom from hurt if we chose to limit the impact of the ego, moving it to a quiet, insignificant place of white noise. It is part of us, but let's make it the tiniest part.

Use the ego, not as a guide telling you anything about you as a being, but for some insight into the deep, often unacknowledged fears that may not have yet surfaced for healing.

VIVIENNE WESTWOOD
Fashion Designer

Wear your clothes like a beautiful second skin, infused with colour, fun and creativity.

Glamour arises within; its call is reflected in our daily clothing. Match the inner spark with the outer design and enjoy unique, expressive authenticity. Design your own way of showing up in this world that is reflective of your love, joy, creativity and beauty. Allow your clothing to nourish you. Invest well in timeless, sustainable fashion that you can love a long time. Our bodies and souls deserve to feel good. How we put together our outfits each day is an underrated and very nurturing form of creativity. Create a daily beautiful and true expression of you for self and others to enjoy. Who do you choose to be today? Who would you like to be tomorrow? Explore the many facets and expressions of yourself through your personal style. Your style evolves as you evolve and need not be defined by age, gender or culture. Be true to yourself and know it is okay to transform any aspect on a whim. Fashion the best version of yourself throughout this life and you will feel good not only in your own skin but also in the clothes you select to adorn your body with. You and your body love to be admired and complimented—receive this gratefully and graciously, also knowing that your opinion counts above all else. If you love yourself and what you are wearing, others will receive this powerful transmission and treat you accordingly.

VIVIENNE'S SOUL MISSION

To breathe life into the mundane.
To explore possibility within established roles.
To create.
To infuse fun into the world through fashion.
To design a unique, soul-led life.
To challenge established norms.

Guidance for today

Find your uniqueness and express it creatively in all your days to foster peace, love and self-worth.

THE CHOICE

Be yourself and change the world, not just your clothes. You are worthy of a decadent, beautiful life. Claim it now. How you represent yourself to the world indicates to others how you like to be treated. Embrace high expectations for self and others.

WALT DISNEY
Cartoonist, Animator, Film Producer

Live and create life through the magic of imagination and play.

Life across time is eternal. The soul is eternal. Creation is eternal. Acknowledge the creator within you. Every moment you are alive you are creating something, whether that be:
- *Your words to make another laugh, or to inspire or teach*
- *The way you seek fun and play*
- *Via the clothes you choose to show up in the world on this day*
- *The meal that you put together for your family*
- *The way you design your home and living spaces*

Acknowledge the power you possess to create.
Acknowledge your creations, both large and small, as part of the way you move through life, hence drawing in more creative power.

As you claim your creative power, you will become lighter as a being, for creativity is great nourishment for the soul. From here, your creativity may connect you even more deeply with your personal sacred contracts and soul missions. Your creations may change your life and those of others, often in unexpected and unprecedented ways. Your legacy will be felt by many, even just in the changes you bring to how another feels, creates or shows up in the world. Your creativity sends waves of change and possibility throughout the entirety of the universe. Creativity and creation are consciousness in motion, to which there is no end. Be and create infinitely and in ways of increasing magnitude to change the trajectory of humanity.

WALT'S SOUL LESSON

To use the power of play, fantasy and imagination to create joy and possibility.
To create across time, place and space.
To envision, to dream.

Guidance for today

See and activate your creative potential to truly live, bringing forth change, adventure and surprise to enhance your life. Enjoy how it flows on to those in your orbit. Anything that makes you smile is a potential gateway to your creativity.

THE CHOICE

Create as you breathe, moment to moment.

WHITNEY HOUSTON
Singer, Actress

Wise one, meet your true, loving self.

Protect your energy and your state of mind. Our minds lead our life so much more than we realise. A healthy mind is vital for peaceful living, which is successful living. Our minds influence our mood. Our mood then influences our energetic and bodily health and the accompanying vibration we have available for creativity. Make mind health your first priority in life and then all else can fall into place, rather than fall apart. We have so much potential and so many gifts and so much love and transformation woven through our soul missions. There are blessings for self and others beyond our wildest dreams if we can move beyond the ego mind into our divine minds. A mind that is governed by our heart and soul rather than the illusionary false ego is the loving presence we need behind our lives. Teach your children how to navigate their minds from an early age, for it is the greatest gift (and beyond any material possession) that a parent can give. You will give your children the gift of their best whole selves. Life needs our best.

WHITNEY'S SOUL MISSION

To use gifts to elevate life.
To sing to create joy for self and others.
To entertain.
To create.
To love.
To heal.
To know self.
To find freedom from fear and ego functioning.

Guidance for today

Address jealousy, envy, anger, self-doubt, comparison, judgement and incessant worry (or any unfavourable reaction) on any occasion as they register in your awareness. Dive deep into what is going on for you underneath these confronting states as they contain great messages. Freedom to be more of yourself is the promise on the other side of your choice to move through emotions. Do not numb these responses (with all the substances that life offers for this cause) because in doing so, we give negative emotions power and a life of their own to grow and infuse our mind with much toxicity. Sit with these emotions. Discover what message they have for you. Forgive yourself for their appearance and, at the same time, congratulate yourself for being willing to take a look. Each time you can receive the truth underneath an emotion, work to change the pattern and release the energy, you take another step away from ego functioning and into your higher-self living. Life is blissful if approached via the higher self. The opposite is true if one remains in ego functioning—it strips the gloss and hinders the missions. Please know that most often your reactions are just an awareness of things that are going on around you ... and not about you. We so often go to 'what's wrong with me that I'm experiencing this emotion?' We are aware beings, and we can't shut off our gifts of awareness, no matter how unpleasant the information may be that we are subconsciously tuning into. It's generally not your stuff, dear one (so please don't keep trying to make it so). It's just your wisdom letting you know what is occurring around you. Let the information just flow through you and then away from you. Approach this process from a 'that's interesting, what do I need to know here?' point of view. Make the incoming information fleeting and therefore gentle on your nervous system. Receive the truth, the information, the message, the energy and move on. You are a free-flowing, powerful being. Don't allow the unpleasant to stick. Focus on feeling your bliss.

THE CHOICE

Befriend your emotions. It's a two-way street. Sometimes the reactions are inner guidance asking you to release a pattern ... or a call for you to open up to more of you. Often, these triggering feelings are just information coming to us from others and not always pleasant. Find peace in this wisdom. Don't resist awareness that will set you free. Look below initial surface responses to the hidden gems of wisdom. Open your journal. regularly asking, 'What is the truth underneath this triggering reaction? Is it mine, someone else's, or a collective vibe I'm picking up?'
It is not always yours, precious one. Hold this truth in your heart to free your mind. Make the demand on self to be free to live a life governed by the higher, unlimited, loving self. My prayer for humanity is an end to senseless suffering, and it starts with you, my friend and co-creator of life.

WILLIAM SHAKESPEARE
Playwright, Poet

Life is a story of our own making.

Life is a stage, and we all have many parts to play. Play your part well as it is all you can do. Life is an unfolding mystery that we co-create with great benevolent forces. Flow with what is occurring to be where you need to be, when you need to be there. Enjoy rather than resist the many interwoven aspects of your life. Our lives regularly interconnect with others; there is quite a dance involved with all the beings that enter our life. Your impact can never be fully known, so use your influence well. Some characters have a large role to play in your life, whilst others have a supporting role. Take notice of who appears in your life. Each individual has a purpose and something to teach you. Open up to this learning with great fervency. There is nothing particularly good or bad in life. Our thoughts determine our response and experience within any scenario. There is great freedom in embracing this truth. Free yourself.

WILLIAM'S SOUL MISSION

To create stories to inspire others to love and dream.
To increase awareness of how life works.
To create, to play.
To explore.
To represent the vast facets of human nature.
To provoke new thought and questioning.

Guidance for today

Cherish all of life. It is so incredibly full of possibility and adventure. Grab hold of life and jump into all of it. There is not a minute to waste. Each moment counts. There is always something to create. Nothing is significant. All is amazing—even the tragic moments that awaken us to more love, if we allow it.

THE CHOICE

Show up for all of your life. Be powerful. Create intentionally and often. Leave a loving imprint on this world. Your legacy lives on, resonating through your lineage and even possibly throughout the ages.

WILLIAM WALLACE
Scottish Freedom Fighter

Hold the vision for a new world.

Sons of the Earth unite. For too long, you have been fighting the wrong fight. Do you not know by now that you are all one and that you have the same grand mission: creating a better Earth now and forevermore? Pull the plug on current patterns of war as they serve no being in the grand scheme of things. It is time to grow up, to awaken, to fight the good fight for the ways of the light. Converting conflict to peace within yourself and then multiplying this on a grand scale involving many beings doing the same is necessary for peace to permeate all of life. Each being's intent to find inner peace counts and is an integral part of all missions. It is embarrassing for us as a world that wars are still raging in modern times. My hope is that the blunders and miscalculations of our forebears are not repeated. It is time for Earth and her beings to evolve, to become more resonant with other higher vibrational planets that have been patiently waiting for eons. As Earth evolves, transmuting darkness into light, the solar system feels the tweaks in creative potentiality.

Awaken, my friend, it is long overdue. It is time to take our rightful place in the cosmos, for the cosmos.

WILLIAM'S SOUL MISSION

> To create freedom within.
> To allow all beings to know freedom.
> To quell fear.
> To invite truth.
> To use power to create change.
> To eradicate darkness in one's personal orbit.
> To experience love.

Guidance for today

Pick your battles wisely. Allow your truth to help you with your choices. Unite and wield your swords of light. Open to your guidance to know when and how to use your power most effectively.

THE CHOICE

Wage war on darkness, beginning with self. When there is no darkness running any individual, there will be no reason or motivation to fight—only create. This is a tall order, but men and women are made of great cosmic, ever-unfolding potential.

ZOE
Animal Guardian

(This is included to indicate that yes, animals have soul missions too).

Nurture all of nature.

I speak for the animals. It is time to connect with animals on a foundation of greater equality. There is much to be learned from animals in terms of how they show up for and respond to life. There is a wisdom bestowed within animals (unique to each species) that is gifted to humans when great connection or appreciation is evident. Reciprocal gifting and receiving unlocks this ancient wisdom: the power of star wisdom and Earth wisdom. When engaging with animals, aim to see what you've been unwilling or unable to see, hear and perceive. Connect with what your animals are here to teach you. Open to more, as you are so much more, and can achieve so much more.

SOME PET SOUL MISSIONS

To teach and practise unconditional love.
To provide healing, joy and nurturing.
To encourage responsibility, kindness and care in young human companions.
To carry and share light.
To transmute fear and suffering into love.
To carry and transmute limiting burdens.
To be a conduit for love.

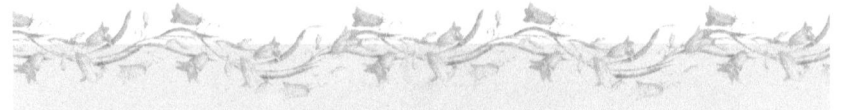

Guidance for today

Connect with your animals through the gaze and the heart. Many pets have soul contracts with you and use cosmic intelligence and synchronicity to find their way into your lives. Your future pets are already imprinted on your soul. Stay aware to receive the signs for guiding them into your lives. The soul missions of your pets are always connected to love, helping you to return to the fullness of your love.

THE CHOICE

Receive the love of your pets and allow this love to infuse your heart and mind. Allow your pets to heal your wounds, nurture and uplift you. They adore you unconditionally and only want you to be happy. They love your love and affection! Gift them your love and, in doing so, learn to become more loving. Gather the force of their love into your very essence and use this magic to transform life into something greater.

WHICH BEINGS ARE SPEAKING TO YOU?

Can you feel the wisdom and light stirring within you upon absorbing the messages you most needed to receive? Do you feel a greater connection to your soul and its purpose? Is there a feeling of something occurring that is just beyond your current periphery of understanding? Can you feel new aspects of yourself opening to the light? Allow these messages to permeate your soul in the upcoming days, months and years. Each time you re-read a contribution, more depth will swirl within your knowing. Increments of change will make their way into your life both subtly and powerfully. Enjoy greater connection with the desire you have for finding meaning, purpose and passion within your life and accompanying soul missions.

I perceive that readers will be given direct access and assistance from our celestial contributors in the form of gifted wisdom and energy to support greater alignment with the next elements of their unique soul missions. This is a text to be re-visited at varying stages of the life journey, hence opening to transmissions as they are required for each new step or trajectory. These amazing beings are accompanying us for the long haul; they see and believe in the grand picture.

Each celestial contributor has not attempted to make the life just lived too significant. I experienced a sacred, humble energy flowing through within their transmissions. Each message radiated an overtone of peace and contained a reflective quality regarding their soul missions. The underlying focus is on the wisdom gained, personal transformation, contribution to the whole, the love experienced and the fear conquered. There was a collective, global feeling coming through rather than a strong individual focus on the specifics of a lifetime. There were many parallels within the soul missions: evidence of oneness, love, healing and the collective desire to contribute and evolve. There is a great desire to share what has been learned. I believe it is part of our soul missions to also share what we have learned for the betterment of others and for our evolving planet of contrasts in these times. I feel like some of these beings have helped save me from aspects of myself, assisting me to unearth the last vestiges (at this point in time) of my unique set of limitations. I feel I have been set free to be more of me. This wisdom has created the feeling of being more ready to meet the world that is designed for me, rather than hide from it, such is the power of embracing our wholeness. I hope this channelled wisdom assists you to heal, connect with your love and return even more fully to your wholeness.

We are all involved in creating the future human and the future world. Mystics, prophets, saints, buddhas, gods, goddesses and guides of all kinds have been showing us the way for millennia. We are finally listening, opening to and embodying the consciousness and accompanying potential that is truly possible.

'To be what we are, and to become what we are capable of becoming, is the only end of life.'
– Robert Louis Stephenson

Part Three

MY STORY, MY SOUL MISSION, TO INSPIRE YOURS

Looking back over my life, I can see that my missions have always been led by inspiration and a desire for inner peace and contentment. When fully backing, supporting and caring for myself, along with avoiding unfavourable influences from the world around me, I have always followed what lit me up—with a healthy dose of intuition interwoven in every life decision. As a child, I was drawn to all forms of creative expression, whether it be dancing, gymnastics, artwork or writing. I loved to move. I loved beauty, magic, surprises and adventures of all kinds. As a young person, I found my adventure within the pages of books (I was a prolific reader) and within my neighbourhood, always planning adventures for my friends. Much of these passions were indicators of future soul missions. I combined my love of learning and books with my career as a primary school teacher. The stresses of this job and my own surfacing wounds then drew me to the healing arts, especially energy healing. Not long after starting my reiki and intuitive guidance business, I received the call to write—teaching and healing in a new way. Even though I had no conscious intention of being a writer, once the possibility crossed my path, its potential wouldn't let go. There was always a niggling feeling that writing was calling and it would not be ignored. I eventually left my lovely teaching comfort zone and haven't looked back. New life was calling and evolving.

New chapters in life can literally begin overnight. One morning, I experienced being in that powerfully insightful time between sleep and wakefulness and received a 'download' complete with many chapter headings for my first book, *'Pearls of Wisdom: For Your Path to Peace'.* I turned to my husband and said, 'I'm going to write a book!'

I expected him to be as shocked as I was, as there was never any consideration on my behalf to become an author. He responded with, 'That's great. Can I have the first signed copy?'

As a side note, I must say that my husband's unwavering belief in me and my work is part of the reason these books are going out into the world and I'm finding the courage to continually show up. Surround yourself with those who believe in your wildest dreams.

Almost within days of receiving my book idea (as if the universe was sending me confirmation that this was all very real), a beautiful client said to me, 'Your words are gold. You should write a book.' It was the willingness to open to the missions that were calling to me that allowed me to open up to my new path as a writer and author.

'Pearls' was my wisdom so far, originating from what I'd experienced in life. It arose out of my desire to no longer be the effect of my emotions, feelings, reactions and suffering. I chose instead to move into the space of receiving the messages within difficult experiences and to allow this wisdom to move me towards peace. Peace was paramount and was all I truly desired.

Many of the themes in 'Pearls' were also inspired by clients and the things we had worked on understanding and unlocking together, further evidence of the interconnectedness of our soul missions. I found that the more I accessed my wisdom, the closer I moved towards my potential and the accompanying requirements for the next stages of my mission. I discovered that peace is essential for accessing the inner wisdom surrounding our missions and the accompanying phenomenal lives. We must connect with our peace to hear our inner guidance despite what goes on around us.

I have always loved learning about what makes me 'tick' and, at the same time, gaining more understanding of how the world works. Each time we learn about ourselves, we grow in self-worth. Self-worth is the foundation for so much as it affects what we are willing to do, have, be, create and receive in life. If we want to get to a greater place in our lives, we need to be willing to change the deeply embedded concepts we carry of ourselves, and that comes from finding our own wisdom and worth because everything we believe about ourselves is showing up in our lives right now. As per the theme of '*Pearls*', 'the world is our oyster and it contains so many pearls' if we are willing to acquire the wisdom to dive deep to retrieve the pearls gifted to us.

The initial writing part of my journey occurred almost spontaneously, although I had been subconsciously preparing for it my whole life. Teaching presented me with 'the world' in terms of the types of uniquely individual limitations that present within us—and an awareness of the accompanying healing that was required. I was constantly writing something as a teacher—gradually crafting my skills. I am sure that whatever work or life situations you are currently engaged in are also preparing you for what is to come.

The next part of my mission required the greatest healing. I was committed to hiding, to not being seen or using my voice anywhere outside my circle. I think for many of us, our ancestral lines contain memories of being harmed in association with speaking up and sharing our message. Even though I was practising using my voice as a teacher, as soon as I would speak publicly to express my opinions in any way, my throat would literally close over and my body temperature would rise. It was ridiculously extreme.

The fearful response never made any sense to me as I liked contributing and there was no foreseeable or perceived negative outcome. When I realised that this response was formed in other lifetimes, echoing down into this one, I could work to release the hold it had over me. Understanding sets us free to change patterns. Healing this wound took decades. Overcoming this irrational response involved a gradual stepping up and showing up that was not going to send my nervous system into a meltdown. First, I started with my Reiki One Jane Holman Facebook page. I posted quotes and then wrote some of my reflections on them. I could not deal with having any photos of me on this page for several years. I was still avoiding visibility and hiding behind my words. I can be somewhat introverted (or extroverted depending on the day and mood) and still face an unwillingness to be regularly seen in some way. However, I held the intent to not allow this 'little quandary' to stop me doing the work I came here to do. My mission contains powerful magic (as does yours) and is woven within the essence of my soul. My missions won't be stopped by limiting choices, such is my commitment to bringing everything that wants to be birthed via me to fruition. The demand I have placed on myself involves leaving this planet feeling empty of any great work. If I am triggered to hide, I counteract this by showing up almost immediately. What demands have you placed on yourself to show up for your missions and the dreams contained within them?

Next, I was called to write *'Seeds of Self-Care: For Love and Serenity'*. Writing this book healed the parts of me that were steeped in fear, thus allowing me to show up and be seen a little more. It allowed my whole life to be interwoven with self-care, primarily by connecting with love and changing how I responded to all of life. My new approach to self-care would help move me towards the power of my love, enabling access to the next stages of my mission—simultaneously creating even more beauty, adventure and abundance.

Upon completion of *'Seeds'*, my daughter was finally successful in her ongoing attempts to urge me to start Instagram to reach more readers and spread some inspiration and light. Instagram has been a great challenge and a huge blessing. I had the wrong sense (and another excuse to avoid showing up) of Instagram being a domain for the young, with women my age expected to be observers rather than participants. I had to work hard on my self-doubt-inducing shadow aspects to overcome this. The positives are that I can now comfortably post photos of myself, indicating that I am beginning to overcome my addiction to hiding. An upside was that posting my messages became so much easier because instead of creating time-consuming graphics as I had done for Facebook, I could post a picture of myself, a snapshot of life with my message accompanying it. Through Instagram, I gave myself permission to embrace all the things I love: fashion, beauty, nature, inspiration, creativity and travel, combined with a healthy dose of not being vested in any Instagram outcomes. Doing the work whenever I felt called to do so and spreading the light (regardless of perceived outcomes) became the focus. The upside was the increase in confidence and kindness to self.

Next along my pathway I was called to write *'Light Ignited: Miracles Unleashed'* as another stage in my evolutionary journey.

This mission involved teaching myself and then others how to become open to the superpower we have within for creating miracles of all kinds. It also required me to accept and open up to the full extent of my channelling ability, bringing information into the world from many cosmic beings, guides, gods, goddesses and mystics. *'Light Ignited'* is about being all that we are: the magnitude of us, stepping into what we are truly capable of, without necessarily knowing what that is. It's jumping into the unknown, anticipating more, being more, opening to more and connecting with the infinite potential of the cosmos to support our endeavours for the highest good. Our missions require us to step into the miraculous unknown and meet our miracle personas often.

Today, my mission involves being a channel once again, bringing information from the celestial world into our world: wisdom for elevating us, our lives, the world, and for helping us to connect with our missions. *'Beyond This World, For This World'* is to encourage acknowledgement of the vast array of missions both personally and collectively that are forming an incredible foundation for moving Earth into a new era. This book also asks us to appreciate the interconnectedness of all missions (past, present and future) in changing life as we know it. Through this writing, we are opening to the possibility of bringing heaven (or your equivalent term) one step closer to Earth.

Stepping up and connecting with the depths of our missions is not easy. It requires deep excavation of our limitations and unlearning much of what we thought was real and true for us. For me, it has involved releasing karma and transmuting a lot of suffering into love. The duress is worth it. The more I show up for my missions, the better I feel. The anxiety that was always a background undercurrent calling me to action is now quieter. My health has improved dramatically. I am inspired, worthy and living a life that I would not have imagined was possible decades ago. The more I show up for my mission, the more life shows up for me. The more I serve, the more gifts and abundance I receive. Life is as willing to serve me as I am willing to serve it. We now make a great team. I know this will be true for you as well. Lean into your healing (and your accompanying expanding missions) and away from all that plagues you.

Accepting your missions will move you one day at a time from fear to love as the universe does everything it can to support us to live with purpose. Trust that the right mentors, literature and inner wisdom will be revealed to you to nurture your willingness to walk new pathways. Your star will continue to rise. What a beautiful, vast, star-filled panorama we are creating together. The night sky has never shone so brightly. The universe at large thrives on our contributions infused with light.

My hope in sharing my journey, minus all the dramas, trauma and disasters (that would be another whole book), is that you are both challenged and inspired to stay open to 'out there' possibilities—and to remain true to your new directions, despite all the pressure, both subtle and obvious, to stay in your current comfort zone. I hope you come to know that all you require is already within you just waiting for you to work through any issues that are getting in the way (only temporarily) of your greatest missions. You are all that is needed for your missions. However, support of the best kind is a welcome gift.

Whatever your soul mission is in life, acknowledge your own story of survival and success, as I have done. Create beautiful stories with you directing and starring in the life you love—stories of empowerment, contribution, love and living on purpose. Life is beautiful, life is tough, life is highs, lows and contrasts. When we start to look at our unease and discontent, we open to the experience of life-changing shifts in our energy and beliefs. We can then expand our perceptions around all of life. Awaken to the truth that we are so much greater than we ever thought possible. Connecting with the bigger picture for our lives and maintaining gratitude for the things that make us uncomfortable (as they reveal to us what we need to heal, acknowledge or open to) is key.

When your amazing life continues to reveal itself to you more and more, be aware of not shaming yourself for the life you are living. Continue to invoke the power of gratitude. Gratitude sends a message out into the universe that what we desire is already happening. It's the ultimate form of stepping into receiving. Powerful you created this life. Own this truth. Perhaps you feel you have more than you should ... or more than many who are equally deserving. Own the kindness you've shown to self, the love you've embraced, the pain you've overcome and the work you've done on yourself to co-create the current life you're enjoying. Share your good fortune, change lives, let others see and know what is possible, and perhaps they may seek more consciousness and accompanying potential. There is no need to hide. Be seen. Show up for life. Be a humble source of inspiration—a source of what else is possible. Do this with gratitude and love in your heart and it will be felt all around you. Be willing to transform life for self and others to make it better than it was. That is our mission.

Our soul missions challenge us, desiring to take us beyond what we can currently see or believe. The new life within our soul missions is calling. Eventually, we will become so aligned with what we are creating and becoming that outside distractions will be an insignificant blur with minimal impact upon us. Hold on! This way of being that we can't quite grasp is closer than we perceive and contains great reward and joy. Reach out, believe and trust in the indescribable unknown wonder that is seeking us. Even though we have little reference point for what is to come in response to our new ways of being, I imagine like me, you can feel this newness and accompanying possibility drawing closer.

You are ready to open up even more to receiving, reflecting upon, and acknowledging your own soul missions. Here are some of my soul missions to further inspire you to perceive your own.

To discover, utilise and share the power of the written word to invoke peace, power, potential, love, healing, truth, awareness and consciousness.
To release, absolve and receive karmic lessons.
To listen, to hear.
To understand, to teach.
To release limitations.
To learn about and experience unconditional love.
To receive.
To escape the bondage of fear.
To be the greatest version of self.
To teach, to create, to write.
To establish a love affair with children's literature and convey this to my students.
To read prolifically to craft understanding and skill in writing.
To pioneer new thinking and approaches to living, being and receiving.
To assist fellow beings to connect with their light and soul missions.
To encourage others to explore their true spiritual nature, potential and gifts.
To transmute fear and suffering into love and peace.
To parent, nurture and love.
To be free to manifest.
To experience joy and enlightenment.
To face and heal shadow aspects.
To travel the globe, receiving soul transmissions and clearings.
To transform the energy of places and people.
To be and share beauty.
To connect with the wisdom and power of nature.
To channel the wisdom of universal source for Earthly living.

A POWER CALL TO CONNECT WITH YOUR SOUL MISSIONS

Today I choose me and my purpose.
I remember who I am and the divine plan for my life.
My soul missions evolve according to the highest good.
My soul missions are co-created and involve free will and choice.
As each new day begins, I joyfully receive my guidance.
I am led to all that supports my soul missions.
I allow life to unfold on life's terms.
I trust my role in the grand design of life.
I am blessed.
All my days are blessed.
All my relationships are blessed.
My soul missions are blessed.
My potential to transform all of life is unlimited.

JOURNALLING DISCOVERY

Breathe, become quiet. Connect with your higher self. Engage in some free flow writing to discover more about your soul missions. You may also like to ask to connect with the energy of your spiritual guidance team and/or the guest contributor that you most resonate with to add further insight to your writing.

Ask: What are my soul missions?

....
....
....
....

Ask: What do I need to claim within me to support my unfolding soul missions?

....
....
....
....

Ask: What small steps can I take today to support my soul mission activation?

....
....
....
....

AFTERWORD

Open to the beyond. Be beyond. Go beyond.

I have much enjoyed being a bridge between the worlds, bringing forth new wisdom from our celestial contributors. I have been deeply inspired and in a state of wonder as to what we beings endure and explore in the name of our own evolution and for that of the collective. We are all superheroes conquering much on a day-to-day basis. We have come to Earth to face any inner darkness and simultaneously nourish the best seeded within us to enhance humanity.

Life on Earth is part of a complex grand design with interwoven threads tying us to other times, places and dimensions. Perhaps we exist not just 'here' but are so powerful that our past, present and future selves co-exist with our spiritual essence. Imagine the wisdom that we have encoded within us awaiting our access. In any case, it is not just about this life. We have been preparing to meet the best of us for lifetimes. Each Earthly incarnation is powerful and purposeful. We are fully aware (in our spiritual essence) of what is involved in the missions we have chosen to embark on for each new life.

The 'great forgetting' that we experience on arrival forces us to connect with love and open to communication with our spiritual guidance team at every turn. Our team understands the blueprint for our lives and possesses an accompanying brief overview of our possible life paths and destinies. This blueprint is only a guide and is always open to modification as it is a free will, co-created life. Embrace the challenge of trusting that often what you are being called to do may not yet exist on the planet in any form ... and all that is happening for you (that may be highly uncomfortable or blissful) is preparing you to meet this new purpose, calling or mission. I remember having a deep sense of knowing that I was here to do something important from around the age of eighteen onwards ... with absolutely no glimpse of what that might be. What do you sense deep within you?

I hope the soul purposes and missions of our celestial guests have helped tweak and shape memories and connections, drawing you to a greater awareness of your own sacred soul missions. Life here is more potent and purposeful than I could ever have imagined. The tapestries of our lives are so rich and our purposes and missions impact not just us but the world and the cosmos beyond. We truly are *all* in this life together. Take great comfort in this truth when life is at its most encumbered. You are never alone, no matter what you are experiencing. The most challenging times are for drawing the most out of us, encouraging us to stay open to more awareness, possibility, power, potential and ultimately love: the universal connector and driving force. May you feel your own force and its ripple effects throughout this precious life and beyond. What is truly possible for you, super being?

Enjoy knowing and trusting that you are fulfilling your mission and leaving a magical legacy behind for all that come after you. You have changed your lineage and contributed to the expansion of life on Earth. Let presence, living from the heart and following what lights your inner fire become instinctive rather than intellectual states of being, thus providing powerful ignition for your soul missions.

Ignite your light, ignite your remembrance and move beyond this world, for this world.

ACKNOWLEDGEMENTS

Thank you from the depths of my heart to the amazing beings who spoke through me for this book. My life felt miraculous (including the challenges) and infused with magic throughout the entire process. I am deeply grateful for all the new locations I was drawn to for writing. Each place somehow became an integral part of opening me more: to receive, understand and therefore best convey the messages. It was a reminder that places contain unique energy and powerful magic. How you each showed up at 'opportune' times in my life to help me experience and feel into your messages was an extraordinary gift. It not only best served the writing process, bringing a new level of authenticity and resonance, but also helped me navigate life and up-level in new ways. Your contributions greatly assisted me to understand and meet my soul missions and serve self and life even more beautifully.

Thank you to my graphics type-setting queen, Nikki Jane. Your work lights me up and makes me love the work even more.

Thank you to Pam Grout, for bringing joy, humour, inspiration and a healthy dose of common-sense wisdom into my spiritual path, supporting my soul missions.

Thank you to my husband and children. Your love and belief in me are the fuel behind many aspects of my missions. Gratitude beyond words and beyond this life.

To my readers, Reiki One clients, Instagram and Facebook followers, so much of this revolves around you and your growth, dreams and desires. I am sure many of our missions are interwoven which is most comforting and encouraging. We are blessed. Our missions are blessed. Thank you for being on this journey with me. Until we meet again ... via words or in person, much love to you all.

ABOUT THE AUTHOR

Jane Holman conducts energy healing, intuitive counselling and life coaching through her business, Reiki One, whilst providing considerate direction and genuine motivation for aspiring writers.

In her fourth book, *Beyond This World, For This World: Celestial Words for Modern Times*, Jane invites us to explore our soul missions' depth and power. Her words hold divine wisdom, flowing gracefully and potently from her earlier three works: *Light Ignited, Miracles Unleashed: A Cosmic Blueprint for Your Miracles, Seeds of Self-Care: For Love and Serenity*, and *Pearls of Wisdom: For Your Path to Peace*.

Jane Holman shines as a luminary. Her offerings harmoniously blend mystical insights and encouragement, transcending boundaries within the nexus of spiritual guidance. Jane's resonance is profound, bridging the realms of the soul and the written word.

Website: www.janeholman.com.au
Instagram: @jane__holman
Facebook: Reiki One Jane Holman

www.ingramcontent.com/pod-product-compliance
Lightning Source LLC
Chambersburg PA
CBHW030251010526
44107CB00053B/1660